Sky Blue Eyes

It's 1970 and my Dad takes me to my first Coventry City match. City have just finished sixth in the old First Division, qualifying for Europe. Little did I know there would be a a mammoth forty eight year wait for another top six finish. This is the story of how boyhood love turned into purgatory and back again. Culminating in a glorious day at Wembley in May 2018. Featuring the many changes that have taken place in that time in football and social culture. From the dark days of hooliganism to the sanitised era of Sky TV. A trip through nearly half a century of under achieving and over believing, seen through Sky Blue Eyes.

In memory of my Dad, a true Sky Blue, who passed away during the writing of this book. Also for the late, John Scallan, loyal CCFC fan and one of Wyken's finest.

With thanks to the many friends I've made through Coventry City and football over the years, some of who feature in the recollections in this book. And a shoutout to the admirable Sky Blue Twitter crew.

Also, thanks to the following bands whose song titles make up the chapters of the book echoing the various era's in CCFC history.

Chicory Tip, David Bowie, Sex Pistols, Joy Division, The Smiths, New Order, James, Oasis, Green Day, The Killers, Coldplay, Snow Patrol, The Enemy.

Chapters

Son of My Father The Early 70's

When I went into my bedroom as a seven year old, I'd look with awe and pride at the two rosettes my Dad had pinned onto the wall. One, the red, white and blue of England, preparing to go to the forthcoming Mexico World Cup as defending champions. The other rosette, the pure Sky Blue of Coventry City. About to play in Europe for the first time.

Having steamed through the lower divisions in the Jimmy Hill era, they'd survived two relegation scraps to finish sixth in their third top flight season. I felt blessed to be born into supporting two such illustrious teams. If only I'd have known, before I had seen a live ball kicked, in nearly fifty years, this would be as good as it would get.

A few months previous I'd seen the first televised game I can recall watching. The notorious 1970 FA Cup Final at Wembley between Chelsea and Leeds United. My Mum's Auntie Elsie and Uncle Bill had a huge colour telly which was rare in those days. They invited me and seemingly half their street around to watch the match. The front room was packed with long haired flare wearing neighbour's clutching beer poured out of mega large tins called the Party Seven.

These were an invention that predated binge drinking. A ridiculously hard to open huge can that inevitably sprayed a good deal of its contents over frustrated boozers in wait. No doubt inviting people to drink seven pints in one sitting would have the health police up in arms these days. But stay at home drinkers were quite happy to have a whole night's supply of ale next to their armchair. It certainly ramped up the mood as the national anthem blasted out from the television set.

The atmosphere was electric. I was hooked. Most of the people present wanted Chelsea to win. Dave Sexton had assembled a stylish artistic side not without a nasty streak, courtesy of serial hitman defender, Ron, "Chopper" Harris. Leeds were a seriously disliked outfit. Some of that was down to jealousy because they were excellent and successful. But a lot of the animosity came from the win at all costs ethos installed into the team by manager, Don Revie.

The pitch was awful, covered in sand. The rivalry between the two sides spilled into a brutal contest, foul after foul, confrontation after confrontation. Years later, a prominent referee officiated the match again on video using a modern interpretation of the rules. He reckoned he'd have awarded about eighteen yellow cards and half a dozen reds. Fittingly for a pitched battle with neither side prepared to yield, it finished a 2-2 stalemate. Chelsea won the replay at Old Trafford.

To me from then on, football seemed great. Passion and spectacle. Grown men of a reserved nature suddenly bursting with raw emotion. One of the blokes I'd encountered at the showing of the Final at my Mum's Auntie's gave me a box of Coventry City football programmes and paper cuttings from their rise up the division's to the top echelon. He said his wife was nagging him to get rid of them. I thought that he must have been seriously henpecked to get shot of such a treasure trove.

I felt like I'd won the pools, as I shifted through the box of recent memorabilia. Programmes seemed a great idea, the line-up's, action pictures, previews, mangers opinions. Football became everything. I just had to see a game. I badgered my Dad relentlessly and he said he'd take me to a match at the start of the forthcoming season. Firstly there was the little matter of watching England on the box as they retained the World Cup.

There was plenty of hype. I used to long for my Dad to fill his motorbike tank up with petrol so I could get my hands on another of the Esso England World Cup coins. Each with the Jules Rimet trophy on one side with the head of an England squad member on the other. I never did get to complete the collection. I was also introduced for the first time to the football song. Called, Back Home, it was a patriotic catchy little ditty about how the lads were flying a great distance across the globe to bring home the sport's greatest prize.

Fat chance. I got my first taste of what was to become a regular dish, having your dreams scuppered by the Germans. But that tournament did contain a gift from heaven, the winning Brazilian side. Playing with a swagger and supreme self confidence in their wonderful abilities they took over England's crown. I was totally smitten now.

On the evening of August 25th 1970, my Father took me to Highfield Road for the first time to see Coventry City play Wolverhampton Wanderers. We sat in the Main Stand, best seats in the house. The aura of a night fixture seemed to make it all the more special. To this day, I still think there is an extra added quality in a midweek encounter played under lights. Like it has something of theatre about it. Cigar smoke wafted thorough my nostrils. Dad pointed to my left and said, "That's where the hooligans watch from."

He was referring to the West End Terrace, situated under a stand. City fans occupied one half separated from rival supporters by a couple of rows of policemen. This struck me as the worst job in the universe. Being a human fence between two mobs keen to do physical harm to each other. The thin blue line struggled to hold firm as the two sets of fans goaded and threatened, fists in the air. It was my first glimpse of football's darker side. There would be plenty more.

Sitting near me there was a guy who appeared to have a megaphone inserted into his mouth. Every few minutes, he'd yell, "Come on you Sky Blues!" at a ear splitting volume that would have given Brian Blessed a run for his money. He never said anything else, looking quite emotionless until breaking once again into his mantra.

I don't recall anything about the action on the pitch other than a Wolves striker called Hugh Curran scoring what proved to be the only goal of the game. As City tried vainly to get back on terms, tears began to stream down my cheeks. It continued on the way home. My Dad said he wasn't going to take me again until I learnt to handle defeat better. This made me even more sorrowful.

The thing is despite numerous experiences of being on the wrong side of results, I've always had a complete aversion to losing. Be it my football team or a knockabout game of pool in the pub. I've always thought winning means everything. Obviously, you want to do it with panache but leaving Highfield Road that night, I could see where Don Revie was coming from.

In his Chelsea player manager days, Rudd Gullit coined the term, "Sexy football". To me, there is only winning football. There is nothing worse than an opposition manager calling you the best team he's come up against all season. It almost always means you're being patronised and have lost.

But now I had a problem. Even if I could become the first young boy to man up and stop my blubbering in defeat, my Dad would not be able to take me to many games anyway. To be precise, none of the Saturday fixtures as his job was manager of a local bookmakers. As such, he had to work on the premier gambling day of the week. I persuaded my Uncle Richard to take me a few weeks later. A drab goalless draw with Huddersfield ensured he wouldn't have to give me loss aversion counselling on the way home.

That was my first experience of the terraces on The Spion Kop, an open undercover end that housed the scoreboard. We got there early so I could stand at the front and get a decent view. To boost chances of this happening, we took a sturdy wooden box for me to stand on.

I also took my rattle. A strange contraption that frequented young hands at grounds in the 50s/60s. It took a mighty effort from a kid to make it whirl round and produce a satisfactory applause sound. A bit like those hideous modern clappers that are in vogue in modern football stadiums to save tourist fans the trouble of putting one paw against the other.

Then Uncle Richard said he didn't want to take me on a regular basis as he, "Didn't really like football". Surely the most incomprehensible words ever uttered. I have always harboured a mistrust in blokes that don't enjoy football like its a character flaw. Women who dislike the game I can understand because some men in relationships take it way too seriously which I did myself for years.

Not liking football just seems like you want it easy. To be immune from the dark cloud of defeat that blights your weekend. Having said that there is a lot about the game I find unpalatable, particularly these days. But I still hanker to know all the results as soon as possible.

One of the best football related television programmes I've ever seen is the episode of comedy, Ripping Yarns, starring Michael Palin as a loyal super fan of an ailing club. Following another humiliating defeat he comes home and smashes his own house to pieces as his long suffering wife tries to save the heirlooms. It perfectly, through hilarious exaggeration, sums up the frustrations involved as something you've anticipated all week turns rotten in front of you once again.

My bugbear became that in those early years, not being allowed to go on my own, I only went to night matches. On a couple of occasions, Coventry played on a Friday evening as a experiment to see if it would counter falling attendances. I'd prayed it would work but it didn't. I felt delighted when a strange midweek competition called The Texaco Cup was introduced. It featured English and Scottish teams who hadn't qualified for Europe. As we crashed out to Motherwell, I managed to quell tears made worse by the fact we'd lost to a Scottish team.

Even when in my first season, we played mighty Bayern Munich in a midweek second leg Fairs Cup tie, it was a forgone conclusion as we'd got thumped 6-1 in the first leg. My second heartbreak at German hands and still twenty years from Chris Waddle's penalty entering space orbit. I was already reeling from not being able to go to Saturday games which had meant I'd missing seeing the Sky Blues score one of the most lauded and famous goals in football history.

Fortunately the Match of the Day cameras were present to capture for posterity, the Donkey Kick. From a set piece just outside the box, midfielder starlet Wille Carr stood right over the ball and using both insteps flicked the ball up in the air backwards for Ernie Hunt to crash a glorious volley over the wall and into the net. The innovative wonder strike won both goal of the month and season.

Any doubts the trick could be repeated were quashed when the move was outlawed from further use as it was ruled, Carr had technically touched the ball twice having used both feet to propel the ball upwards. But the goal stood on the day and still gets many hits on YouTube due to the BBC presence that afternoon. It's a move any of that feted 1970 Brazilian team would be proud of.

In truth, such moments were in short supply during my formative years. City followed up the European qualifying season by finishing a respectable tenth. But goals were hard to come by. They scored only 37 times conceding just one more. Noel Cantwell began to attract criticism for the dour style of play. The following season results began to worsen and gates dropped further. Towards the end of the campaign with relegation fears looming, Cantwell was sacked.

Caretaker Bob Dennison kept the club up. Following the legendary one off, Jimmy Hill, into the manager's office was always going to be a difficult task for Cantwell. But in fairness, he led the club to Europe. An achievement many other coaches in later years were hired to emulate without succeeding. What many felt the Sky Blues needed was a big name. Rumour persists to this day the club approached Brian Clough.

What the fans got was something of a compromise. A "dream team" of experienced Joe Mercer as general manager with the unproven Gordon Milne as team boss. Mercer made his name in management partnership with Malcolm Allison at Manchester City. Genial Joe proved the perfect foil for the exuberant Allison at Maine Road during a golden era for the blue Mancs. Milne after a solid playing career, the highlight being well over 200 Liverpool appearances, was marked down as a promising young boss after doing well at non league Wigan.

It didn't take long for the duo to work out the fans at Coventry were crying out for an entertainment factor at the club. To this end, two signings were made, one, Colin Stein from Glasgow Rangers, a forward of considerable reputation and prowess. He quickly became a firm favourite with supporters. His bravery was captured when Stein was pictured standing on one leg in front of the West End after scoring a goal after he'd insisted on playing on when injured.

The second addition would make trips to watch Coventry far more enjoyable for myself and others for years to come. A gangly winger by the name of Tommy Hutchison signed from Blackpool where he had played with Milne. A player of great skill, masterful in dribbling and ball control he soon became a great favourite with the fans.

It seemed most clubs in that era had an almost pop star like ball player. Names like Frank Worthington, Tony Currie, Stan Bowles, and of course George Best. Mavericks who could change and influence a result in an instant with an inspirational piece of skill. Now City fans had their own such hero, affectionately known as Hutch.

Early on he scored what many who were present describe as the best individual goal by a City player. A stunning run from his own half at Highbury through a gauntlet of Arsenal players. Unfortunately, I've never seem the goal and am not sure that footage exists from days long before blanket TV coverage of every piece of vital action.

Another boost arrived when I found a few of my friends of a similar age to myself were being allowed to attend matches without their parents. I pleaded with my Dad to let me go with them.

"Ok then but be careful." I was ecstatic.

Lads I particularly remember from my initial parent free trips to Highfield Road were, Dave McMenemy, Ray Gower, and Steve Collins. We were all City nuts and would get to the ground as soon as the gates opened to ensure our place at the front near to the goal in the Kop. Sometimes that meant two hours to kill in often freezing weather before the action started.

Catering at matches was a lot more primitive than today. A hut at the back of the terraces while around the pitch's sanded surrounds, a chap walked round with what resembled an oversized tea urn attached to him. Also doing laps of the perimeter walked the pie seller, the holy grail of football supporter treats if your budget ran to it.

"It's actually hot!" You'd very occasionally yell with glee on the rare occasions the pie didn't have the texture of a cold sparsely meat filled sponge. If you were particularly patient there were hot dog sellers outside on the way out of the ground. These tasted even more delicious if scoffed on the back of a home win.

Halcyon days. The proximity of the ground to where we lived in Stoke Aldermoor meant we could be home in time for tea and to watch Doctor Who on telly. If you didn't hear all the other results at the stadium after the game ended, the only real way to catch up on the day's news was to buy the Saturday night Pink edition. This was printed by the main local press outlet, the Coventry Evening Telegraph.

It's arrival at the newsagent's around six o'clock was eagerly awaited. Queues would form particularly if the Sky Blues had achieved a positive result. The front page would feature bold headlines reflecting the afternoon's outcome together with an in depth attack by attack summary of the game. More so of the first hour or so with deadlines tight. Late score updates would just say for instance, "Then United levelled matters with two minutes to go through so and so."

A full results service, latest tables and a comprehensive round up of local sport completed the Saturday night's essential reading matter. A darts or dominos player from the local social club would be thrilled to find their name in the same edition of a rag that had the latest exploits of household names at Highfield Road.

Every town had its equivalent of The Pink. The name and colour would vary slightly from locality to locality, for instance, The Green Un. Teletext and Ceefax, more television channels, then the Internet and social media eventually spelt the death keel for these legends of sporting print. The fastest way to gather the day's vital football info had become positively tortoise like. Gradually the titles were axed, another victim of "progress".

The next weekend football delight was Match of the Day which featured highlights of just two fixtures. It produced an extra buzz walking up towards the ground of your team and seeing the BBC vans outside setting up to film the game. You wanted your club to do well even more, so national exposure greeted a positive result and performance. The opposite saw reason for a rare early Saturday night in bed.

ITV featured regional football on a Sunday afternoon. In our case in the Midlands, Star Soccer, with commentary from Hugh Johns. Johns had a genial understated sense of excitement as he relayed his comments. He commentated live on the 1966 World Cup Final for the channel, only to be forever overshadowed by the legendary, "They think it's all over" cry from Kenneth Wolstenholme over on the Beeb.

Nowadays, games have two sometimes even three match navigators sitting on the gantry. The action rarely gets to speak for itself. The great commentators of the 70's like John Motson, Barry Davies and Brian Moore knew where to leave gaps, let the pictures breathe and do the talking without unnecessary verbal ramble.

Star Soccer had extended highlights of one game in the Midland complete with some of the lower key boring bits.

Then there came potted action, goals and near misses from two other matches in other regions. I used to envy some of the other areas that had less clubs thus increasing their chance of being shown. The Midlands is home to a lot of teams so those who picked the fixtures for televising were spoilt for choice.

Having said that, we used to joke the programme always ended with the statement, "Star Soccer will be back next week from somewhere in Derby." due to the amount of times the cameras visited the Baseball Ground. In fairness, under Clough then Dave Mackay, Country were the Midlands premier club winning the league twice, once under each mentioned boss.

"Going up the City." was the phrase used to describe a visit to Highfield Road. And on January 27th 1974, a remarkable forty thousand plus crowd turned out to witness Derby visit Coventry for an FA Cup Tie. The special gate marked a special occasion, Sunday football. Playing on the sabbath had long been a strict taboo. But the authorities relented as due to industrial disputes, power cuts were commonplace. Floodlight use became banned as a result.

This led to early kick-off's and with electricity thought to be less in demand on Sunday's, some clubs asked to play on that day. Due to observances rules, admission by tickets was prohibited. Entry by programme purchase became the method used to get around the somewhat archaic laws that had stood for decades, in some cases centuries.

Playing on such an unusual almost sacred from football day caused a lot of excitement. Walking up to the ground with Ray, his Dad and the hordes, my sense of anticipation and history heightened. Police on horseback milled round keeping order. Then a lad walking towards the stadium did one of the stupidest things I've ever seen. He put his cigarette out by stubbing it against a police horse's backside.

Not surprisingly the equine creature went ballistic, front hooves up way in the air, swirling around as the constabulary uniformed jockey held on for dear life. Policemen arrived to try and calm the animal but thought better of being on the end of a kicking from a metal horseshoe. The crowd scattered in fear. As the story went round inside the ground, hearsay had it they took the horse into the nearby canal to cool down.

We couldn't get near the front and my entire experience of the game was one where my main view became of grown ups backs and shoulders. Occasionally a gap appeared and I glimpsed a segment of the pitch, the odd player. A moment of excitement or near miss was indicted by a frightening body surge where you finished up about fifteen yards from the place you had originally stood. Those moments were maybe thankfully few and far between as the match ended goalless.

The frustration of not being able to see led us to decide to sit down for bigger games in the budget priced Main Stand Enclosure. Just above pitch level, a row of luxury boxes as they were termed had been built. Looking like slightly lavish wooden beach huts with long windows, each unit had a mounted telly fitted in and food served. A long way from corporate entertainment but quite impressive back then.

Underneath there was an unassuming three rows of Sky Blue seats. This is where we plumped to watch some of the games from when we thought we might not get to the front of the terraces. The bonus being you could sit right by the players tunnel and watch them emerge from darkness into the cauldron of action. But I've never sat anywhere so cold.

During some winter games it seemed like I'd lost the feeling in my feet.

The power cuts did me one disservice. To conserve electricity, some home cup games were played during daytime in midweek. This being while we were at school. The teachers cottoned on, warning about absence without necessity. My Dad said I had to adhere to this. Now to me, while education is of great importance there is no greater learning necessity than seeing you team play in a vital cup tie.

Thus I became marooned in a classroom learning such non essentials as maths and English while the Sky Blues fought out a home draw with Man City in the League Cup Quarter Finals. As recompense, Dad said I could stay up to watch the replay when it was televised on Sportsnight. The programme was BBC's midweek sporting slot which usually consisted of boxing and football with the odd diversion like showjumping.

The thing was, how would I avoid finding out the score so I could view the highlights as if it were a live match? This task is famously mirrored in a marvellous episode of, Whatever Happened to the Likely Lads. Bob and Terry are desperate to avoid learning the result of a competitive England fixture in Bulgaria so they can watch the highlights like a real game. Increasing their plight is fine Yorkshire actor Brian Glover who bets them that they'll hear the final score.

The duo seek all sorts of sanctuary from him including inside a church. Then comes the punchline of the match being fogged off, hours before as they sit down to watch the delayed transmission. My own personal effort lasted until just before I left school for the day. Some lad had sneaked a radio in and shouted, "We lost 4-2!"

He's probably now a professional spoiler, the type of bloke who tells his kids the endings to classic films as they watch them for the first time. I remember the presenter, David Coleman saying what a great game it was and how both teams could be proud. It just felt like the being patronised feeling I described earlier. Who takes joy from losing in a classic and being football's equivalent of a bridesmaid?

Going to games with your mates brought a great sense of bravado, like you were finally growing up. A sense we had our own little gang. A feeling of belonging acted as a kind of Dutch courage in what were dark days for trouble on the terraces and outside the ground. Speak to anyone over the age of fifty now about their early days of attending football and they'll casually reel off a host of hooliganism related stories. It was so commonplace you just accepted it as occupational hazard.

As kids we were mainly left alone although there was the phenomenon of the scarf snatcher. Just as soldiers used to steal medals off opposing troops their side had killed, thugs would take a scarf from an opposition fan like a badge of honour. But some would just pick on a little kid, bully them into handing over the scarf. Then like a Fishermans tale, spin the yarn it was acquired after a full blooded one on one with the other mob's top boy.

"Give us your scarf." became the last words you wanted to hear. Nobody with pride and passion in their club surrenders their colours easily. However, when faced with a kicking from somebody twice your size there isn't that much of an option. The obvious alternative option was not to wear a scarf. But this indicated you favoured a cowardly cop-out above club loyalty.

In those days, replica shirt wearing fans were few and far between. Certainly not the massive income generating commercial moneymaker it is for clubs today. This may have been because there wasn't that much money about. In working class communities, strikes and lay-off's were a regular occurrence. Most people showed their allegiance with a scarf or bobble act that mirrored their budget.

Metal badges also gained popularity. A good inventive affordable way of showing your support. Badges usually featured various variations on the club crest. Some were more humorous or off centre poking fun at rivals. The best boost if you've got a decent history is a badge alluding to major trophies you've won.

One quirky fan fad emerged in the mid 70's. The cotton patch which you would sew onto your scarf, jacket, even trousers. I purposely aggravated a small rip in a pair of jeans then suggested a Cov City patch as a means of repair to my Mum. Cheaper than a new pair. She readily agreed. A lot of the patches were tacky and the one I chose was no exception. A two fingered salute signalling victory or erm, something else above the name, Coventry. Well, it was purchased from the heartland of sophisticated merchandise, Blackpool.

Clubs hadn't really latched onto the fact they were sitting on a highly marketable brand. I think Coventry were one of the first clubs to appoint a commercial manager. Others soon followed suit. Copyright remained lax with the penny slow to drop that a simple thing like the club crest could be a powerful tool of commerce and potential income. Image rights were decades away from being heard of.

I did get my first replica kit for my birthday during the 1973-74 season. City had a variant on their traditional Sky Blue design with the shorts being black which also appeared as shirt collar and sleeve trim. I felt proud when playing football in the kit at school in games lessons like I was representing the club.

Over the years though I never took to wearing replica tops mainly due to the advent of sponsorship. My love of football kits died somewhat when the names of companies started appearing on the front of tops. Around this time the price of kits seemed to rise steeply. I felt like fans were shelling out to advertise someone else's product that they didn't care a jot for. Surely that can't be right.

Around this time, I also obtained a weird pair of football boots. I asked my parents for some new boots for Christmas. As I excitedly tore off the wrapping paper and opened the box, I received a surprise on examining the new boots. At the base, there were two screw in studs at the front, nothing unusual there. But at the back, mounted on a axis, there were four more studs that span around a full 360 degrees.

If memory serves, they were endorsed by Spurs and England star, Alan Mullery. The idea seemed to be the studs moved when you moved, gliding through the mud, giving greater balance. This would-be groundbreaking notion had one major drawback, it was bollocks. What would happen was, you'd do a sharp turn and as if you were on a playground roundabout go flying ending up face down or on your backside.

Around the time there used to be a comic book football story called Billy's Boots. It featured a young lad, hapless at football who acquired a pair of old boots that formerly belonged to an ace striker. Somehow they magically enabled the lad to play in the same formidable style as their original owner. If that could happen, my boots belonged to Norman Wisdom or a circus clown as I spent the majority of games flying through the air.

The 73-74 season petered out into a lower half finish for the Sky Blues. Nothing special but the season was for me. My first campaign going to games independent of family. Experiencing the togetherness of friends, the excitement of hacking it without an adult's guidance. We'd got our own idol at last in Tommy Hutch. In what were grim times of power shortages and little money, we'd found our own little oasis in, "Going up the City".

Golden Years The Mid 70's

The summer of 1974 brought more international disappointment as England had failed to qualify for the World Cup to be held in West Germany. A situation magnified by Scotland reaching the finals. This downer became offset somewhat by my discovery of one of the joys of any young fan, even to this day. Collecting the football sticker.

The Panini album I had was very impressive and also very empty. Setting about rectifying this, I spent every spare penny on packets of stickers. Kids would huddle on street corners holding impromptu swap shops. Rare stickers became a powerful tool of currency. You could swap as many as twelve stickers or more for one that you highly desired and required to complete your collection.

Just like the Esso coins, I fell short in my quest to complete my album, being envious of those who filled their book. The tournament was enjoyable though. In the absence of England, I began rooting for the Dutch. The Netherlands had a style of play I found bold and fascinating. Termed total football, the idea was to keep possession, wearing out the opposition before breaking them down with a deadly sudden upping of pace.

I particularly worshiped Johan Cruyff. That summer holiday on the playing fields of the Aldermoor, I modelled myself on the laid-back but devastating artistry of Cruyff. In truth, I had the long hair but little other of the maestro from Holland about me. It galls to say, despite spending much of my youthful spare time with a ball at my feet, at best I was only a slightly above average footballer.

This wasn't helped by changing my favoured position regularly. Tommy Hutch, on the wing one week, Cruyff in the middle the next. I also really liked going in goal. I've always had a soft spot for the keeper. A position where you can perform many heroics but one slip makes you the villain. My fascination with the man between the sticks increased when a young Scottish goalkeeper called Jim Blyth broke into the Sky Blues first team.

A brilliant shot stopper with great reflexes and masterful at one on one's with an opposing player clean through on goal. Injury prevented Blyth from joining Manchester United and he was never quite the same afterwards. I had many a happy hour flinging myself through the mud in the local parks. But crosses were my Achilles heal. And for a keeper, that is a major deficiency.

I also enjoyed, as do most youngsters, playing up front. The glamorous job, hitting the net and taking the glory. Again, I had a glaring weakness. For a tall lad, I was rubbish in the air. Having an almost phobia like fear of the hardness of football's didn't help. Back then, footballs were cased and heavy. You had to get a header spot on or suffer the consequences.

In recent years, there has been a lot of debate about whether heading old style heavy footballs has led to dementia. The most high profile study being that of West Brom striking legend, Jeff Astle. There is certainly compelling evidence and you feel for families who have suffered the premature loss of a loved one while medical arguments rumble frustratingly on.

My dislike of heading the old footballs wasn't helped by the fact I rarely got chance to improve. Although me and my friends spent every spare minute kicking a ball it wasn't very often a fully inflated proper ball. For they didn't last long before bursting, often victim of the metal security spikes on the roof of the local club as we played in the car park. Not being able to afford to replace it we played on with the now airless smaller ball.

We even used a tennis ball if needs must and there were no other orb alternatives. On one occasion at school, bereft of any kind of ball, me and Ray invented stone football which is self explanatory. Kicking around the biggest, roundest pebble we could find. It became quite a cult game in the playground before being outlawed by teachers on health and safety grounds in maybe the first ever example of PC gone mad.

If anyone had a brand new ball, they would instantly become everybody's sudden best mate. Word would go round that a lad had purchased a ball. Everyone would turn up on the patch of the estate where he played in the hope of getting a game with decent equipment for a change.

Even then it was rarely a proper professional standard ball but rather a lower weighted lighter replica one. Usually covered in black and white hexagons with the names of the First Division clubs on the white bits. Given a half decent whack, these things flew a mile and it wasn't long before they ended up on a rooftop or impaled on one of the dreaded spikes.

If it was raining too much to play outside then we went around somebody's house and played the next best thing to real football, Subbuteo. Unless you had a decent sized table which we didn't, it was virtually impossible to find a big enough flat surface on which to mount the baize pitch. The accessories such as TV tower, scoreboard even floodlights were much sought after.

Every year the new Subbuteo catalogue was issued for free. We'd rush up to the shop to get one and spend ages mulling over the kits, deciding which team we'd get next. Players would often pick up injures of rather lose their base, even a leg and become a passenger courtesy of some hastily applied glue. The games were always fiercely contested. Purists became adept at the flick to kick correct method of manoeuvring the players, with anyone using the frowned upon drag movement like myself being chastised as a cheat.

At the age of around nineteen in one desperate attempt to avoid adulthood, me, Ray and a few other lads formed a Subbuteo league. Partly I suppose to fill in midweek nights when we couldn't afford to go to the pub. A group of us would go to the house of a mate called Stephen Gardner, our host with a big pitch and table in the spare bedroom. We'd all take our own teams and play the week's fixtures.

Ray was newly married at the time. His wife's face a picture as he announced he had to go out for a vital game and walked out to his car carrying a little boxed Subbuteo team. During one match Ray got overheated and trashed the players. Stephen typed out a letter from the league's imaginary hierarchy threatening disciplinary action and posted it to Ray's house. His wife must have been stunned when that dropped through the letterbox.

My anticipation for the 1974-75 season couldn't have been greater. I started secondary comprehensive school not long after and hated it with a passion. Weekends became even more eagerly awaited. Unfortunately the season got off to a dismal start as we went the first eight matches without a win. This was only the tip of the iceberg as the club were plunged into financial troubles that would plague us for years to come.

In August, Coventry paid a huge fee by their standards of £240,000 for highly rated Liverpool defender Larry Lloyd.

The plan being to offset the outlay by selling two players to Tottenham for around the same money. But the sudden departure of Spurs longstanding boss, Bill Nicholson scuppered the deal. City had spent a lot of money that they did not have.

To make matters worse, Lloyd was plagued by injury during his time at the Highfield Road and we never saw the best of him. Nobody seemed particularly sorry a couple of years later when he departed for a much smaller sum to Nottingham Forest. Then, hey presto! Larry became the central defensive kingpin in Clough's side that incredibly won the First Division at the first time of asking and the following season, the big one, the European Cup.

Our form picked up but it became the birth season of a sell to survive template that persists at Coventry to the present day. The club again attempted to recoup their money by selling Willie Carr to Wolves only for the deal to collapse on medical grounds. I rated Carr highly so this pleased me. But eventually he did depart to Wolverhampton for much less than originally agreed. He went on to play a good few hundred games in gold and black with no sign of any great injury.

Joe Mercer had moved "upstairs" to become a director so it must have been tough for Milne. We did end up with a decent home record which always boosts the morale of the regular attendees. I also went on the West End Terraces for the first time. Home of our more unruly fringe, my Dad had said. I enjoyed it. The fans in the there seemed more vocal and there was a good atmosphere. But the excitement of Division One football had given way to harsh fiscal realities.

Because of this the next season would be difficult. Although it started well with a storming 4-1 win at Everton. By this time I'd befriended a lad who lived by us called Lawrence

Murphy. A fanatical Manchester City fan whose favourite player, Francis Lee had now departed to Derby. Lawrence persuaded me to go in the Main Stand Enclosure for our opening game against reigning champions,The Rams.

When the players were inspecting the pitch before the game, Loz, as we called him for short, legged it onto the grass and asked Lee for his autograph, of which he obliged. I joked I expected Franny to fall over in reference to his reputation of winning more penalties than any other player.

Lawrence had the same love as football as me and we played on any suitable surface we could find, day and night. For some mad reason, our chosen game was one against one, often on a full sized pitch. God, we must have been fit. I must have had my capacity of hatred for losing tested too as Lawrence was highly talented with a ball at his feet and beat me more often than not.

I did manage to get bragging rights when we held Derby to a draw before beating Man City at home a few days later. The season turned into another run of the mill lower end of the table affair. But in December 1975, uproar ensued as the club announced plans to sell midfield star player, Dennis Mortimer to nearby rivals Aston Villa. The local paper printed letters night after night complaining about the decision to let Mortimer sign for a club just up the road. The Coventry board cited the difficult financial situation but a lot of fans saw it as lack of ambition.

This was the first time since being in Division One, City had parted controversially with one of the best players because of necessity to pay the bills. The situation would be repeated numerous times down the years. When Jimmy Hill returned to the club in a boardroom capacity, he used the term, "Sell to survive."

No doubt this was to illustrate the gravity of the position the Sky Blues were in. But that is of little consolation to the fans as they watch a player they have nurtured, been patient with when inexperienced, deliver his best work for others. Like Lloyd, Mortimer too would lift the European Cup. You didn't begrudge him or the other departed players who went onto success elsewhere but it did leave a bitter taste.

Being a regular at home matches, I now became more adventurous and yearned to do a away game. This was achieved at the end of January when me and Lawrence travelled to Derby. I felt overawed standing behind the goal in the away section. The Baseball Ground was a noisy old school stadium. Home fans banged their wooden seats to create more of an intimidating atmosphere and got a 2-0 win as reward for their raucous endeavours.

A couple of months later I sat on the back of my Dad's moped as we went over to St Andrews for the local clash with Birmingham. I considered myself now a home and away proper supporter. But the problem with that is finance. My parents did loads for us but weren't particularly well off to put it mildly.

It was to this effect, I managed to bag myself a paper round. The newsagent said I could deliver the papers late on Saturdays when the City were at home but now of course I couldn't go to away games anyway. But me and Steve Collins did decide to go and watch the players pre season training out at Ryton, a fair old hike from our houses in the Aldermoor.

Armed with the obligatory pop and crisps one morning in the red hot summer of 1976 during the school holidays we set off to find the training ground. Despite going prepared with a local folding atlas, due to my dire map reading skills, we ended up in a country village miles away from our intended destination.

Our second mission was more successful and it was fascinating watching the players being put through their pre season paces. None of today's covert private training existed then and you could approach the players afterwards for autographs and photos. You felt the long walk out to Ryton brought a reward of close proximity and insight into your idols preparation practices.

I remember going to Ryton with Lawrence Murphy once to get some photographs signed. Unbeknown to me he'd craftily drawn swasitkas on a couple of the players foreheads. Their eyes nearly popped out of their heads on seeing their image complete with Facist embellishment. I never twigged on until it was too late and they looked upon me like I was an evil closet Nazi.

The club now imbedded in a cost cutting culture bought some excitement to the fans early in the season. Three players were brought in. We were in the buying seat for a change. In hindsight, it had to be one of the best weeks for incoming player business in Sky Blue history. The highest profile name was Terry Yorath from Leeds. The captain of Wales and a robustly competitive hard tackling defensive midfielder.

The other two were relatively unknown. Bobby McDonald joined from Aston Villa. A skilful left back who raided down the flank to supplement the attack and also well capable of scoring goals. The third acquisition meant little to most City fans. Forward Ian Wallace brought from Scottish club, Dumbarton, a flamed hair forward. Not particularly quick but with astonishing positional sense in front of the posts. He would go on to be one of the most popular players in CCFC history.

As with everything Coventry all was not plain sailing at first. Results were mixed but looked likely to end in the comfort zone. Then just as Wallace was making a real impression he received a horrific freak injury at Norwich suffering a detached retina eye injury. The team looked to have potential but as always lacked consistency. This wasn't helped when during a wet winner there were a large number of home games postponed at Highfield Road due to pitch drainage issues.

Eight away games were played on the trot yielding only five points. From a position of seeming safety, City were suddenly sucked into a scrap for survival. The backlog of games meant a row of midweek home fixtures. Only two were won. The last match entertaining Bristol City loomed ever larger as the crunch clash. So it proved.

I'd never been so nervous in my life and got into the West End well over an hour before the evening kick-off. There was an added ingredient. Sunderland were also deep in the drop mix having looked doomed before a nine match unbeaten run. They were at Everton. One from three had to go.

The crowds honed in en masse at Highfield Road. The decision came to delay the start. When things finally got underway the tension was almost unbearable. Thankfully, Tommy Hutchison played one of the many great games of his life scoring twice to put Coventry within touching distance of safety.

But it's never that simple in the Sky Blue universe. Two goals were conceded. All level. Around the ground, ears pressed against transistor radios. A roar went up from both sets of supporters. Everton had won 2-0. If it stayed the same at Highfield Road both teams were safe and the Wearsiders were gone.

If the players didn't know, they did when the final score at Goodison Park flashed onto the scoreboard. With still fifteen minutes to go an extraordinarily scenario took place. The winner takes all blood and thunder clash gave way to an amnesty. Neither side tried to tackle let alone score. The ground went wild at the farcical scenes. The final whistle went. Both clubs were safe and Sunderland down.

To this day, there is extreme sourness in the red and white part of the North East about what happened that night. Events two decades later at White Hart Lane would make things even worse. Jimmy Hill got the blame that May night in 1977. For delaying the kick-off, for the announcement of the result at Everton. It's rumoured in Sunderland, JH even started the Iraq War.

For my part, the start had to be delayed. There were still thousands trying to get into Highfield Road. If the game had got under way on time, numerous fans could have been seriously hurt in the rush to gain admission. We saw later sadly, tragically where this can lead. Football isn't worth the risk of injury or loss of life.

Undoubtedly, flashing up the score was gamesmanship of the highest order or lowest for the eternally resenting Sunderland supporters. But the noise of the whole crowd reacting to radios would have surely got through to the players who would have realised it was game over at Goodison. Personally at that time I didn't care less. The Sky Blues were safe. The future spelt another season in Division One. The selective interpretation of history is the province of the bitter.

Pretty Vacant The Late 70's

For the football supporter, pre season optimism rides high no matter how the previous campaign panned out. So despite the narrowest of escapes I had high hopes for 1977-78. My excitement was further buoyed by becoming a season ticket holder for the first time. £10, hard saved through my paper round brought me entrance to every first team and reserve game too. I plumped for the West End in line with most of my mates. But you could also access the Sky Blue terraces along the side of the pitch under the similarly named stand if things got too chaotic behind the goal.

You had to provide two passport style photos. One for the club's records and one to be stuck on the back inside page of your season ticket. Slow to catch on to the punk mantra, long hair was taboo, I looked like a sunburnt cross between Jimmy Osmond and The Ramones.

I mention punk because it had really captured my imagination by then. 1977 was the summer of the Sex Pistols with their anti Silver Jubilee song, God Save The Queen, only being denied the number one slot by the biggest fiddle in chart history. When the new season kicked off at home on a sunny August day against Derby, punks growing popularity was reflected by the number of spiked haired straight trousered wearers in the West End.

A feeling had emerged that there had become a clarion call for change. That the groundswell was shifting to something new, raw and exciting. This was reflected by Gordon Milne's Sky Blues who beat the Rams 3-1 in a scintillating display of attacking football. Bringing in Ray Graydon as an orthodox right winger, with Hutch on the left, City launched into a brave and bold 4-2-4 formation.

The idea being to bring the best out of the Mick Ferguson/ Ian Wallace central striking partnership. It certainly worked as the duo formed a deadly almost telegraphic alliance. Like they could read the other's next move. This resulted in some of the football ever seen by the home side at Highfield Road. The league season harvested 75 goals, 41 of them bagged between the dynamic duo.

Manchester City came to town and a thrilling 4-2 outcome in Coventry's favour saw a nine match unbeaten run take Milne's revitalised side into the top four. That came crashing down in the manner only Cov can with a 6-0 thrashing at Goodison Park. But it proved a temporary blip. We were now a match for anyone as proved in a League Cup tie at Anfield.

Despite the shock ascending star of Clough's Forest, all conquering Liverpool were still the yardstick to measure a team against. In a red hot atmosphere in front of The Kop, City came away with a two all draw. The replay became one of the most highly anticipated home games in years. Packed like a sardine in the West End, I winced as Jimmy Case hit one of the hardest shots I've ever seen past Blyth to put the Reds ahead.

If the net hadn't been in the way, the power with which he struck the ball would have taken someone out behind the goal. Liverpool won 2-0 but the Sky Blues had shown they were now nobody's mugs. As proven in the very next home fixture, on paper an unassuming festive clash with Norwich which would go down into City folklore.

With a back four decimated by injuries, Milne decided more than ever, defence would be the best form of attack. The Canaries brought into it on a rain sodden pitch which saw

Coventry win by the odd goal in nine. As if that wasn't enough, Wallace scored with a stunning overhead kick and Blyth saved the day with a last minute penalty game. Decades later it remains the best game I have ever seen.

There were plenty more excellent performances to savour. Yorath in midfield added a steel previously lacking while McDonald in marauding full back mode was a revelation. Blyth produced some marvellous stops. A few bad results meant the home game with Nottingham Forest had so much riding on it. A point for Clough's men would sensationally clinch them the league in their first season back in Division One.

A tense and exciting game ensued with everything but goals. Most of the stadium thought Ferguson had scored with a close range header only for Peter Shilton to somehow turn the ball over the bar. A mass pitch invasion greeted the final whistle. This turned nasty with pockets of rival supporters fighting each other. Typical of an era when even in moments of celebration the spectre of hooliganism loomed large. City would only secure European football of their own volition if they won at Bristol City. Despite a mighty away following it ended one apiece.

There was a second chance. If red hot favourites Arsenal beat Ipswich in the FA Cup Final we would still be in Europe. Usually, I'd want the underdogs to win but not as I sat in front of my telly that day. But disaster, as the boys from Suffolk deservedly lifted the trophy at Wembley. I felt as gutted as The Gunners.

Coventry merited something from that season. In the end, maybe we conceded too many in a side given to attack. But there were a lot of games that would live in the memory, much pride to the way we had gone in twelve months from relegation strugglers to Euro contenders. A lot of credit went to Milne for his offensive gamble. But it would be remembered fondly as the Fergie/Wallace season. On the surface an oddball combination, on the playing surface unplayable.

Such was my keenness, I saw every reserve game played at Highfield Road that season as well as all the first team fixtures. The second string usually played home games on Tuesday nights. In one way they were more enjoyable because the result didn't matter so much. It was more laidback and you could have a laugh with your mates.

There were some remarkably high scoring reserve matches around this time. One saw Gary Birtles finish on the losing side despite scoring a hat trick for Forest's stiffs. This saw him elevated to the first team and national prominence when he scored a goal that helped end the reign of Liverpool as two on the bounce European champions. Anyone doubting the value of reserve team football would be silenced by that example.

Lawrence Murphy came to a lot of these fixtures with me. At half time he would perform his party trick of going into the large refreshments mall in the Main Stand and slyly letting off a stink bomb. People would flee the room holding their noses and we'd get straight to the front of the queue for coffee.

The start of the 78-79 season brought much anticipation for building on what we'd achieved in the previous campaign. Myself and Steve Collins decided to move our season tickets to the seats in the West Stand above the behind goal terraces. Some of our other friends were surprised saying there wasn't as much atmosphere sitting down. True but we just wanted the best view we could afford.

Things started well despite a shock League Cup defeat at Chester. Four out of the first six league games brought victories but the season turned into one of frustration. Ferguson suffered a succession of injuries playing only 17 matches and captain Yorath had similar issues and managed only a couple more. Rather than spend a significant amount of money to push on and consolidate the 7th position finish, youngsters were promoted to the senior team

Two decent transfer in acquisitions were made. The first was Steve Hunt from New York Cosmos. An Englishman with a tireless work rate and cultured left foot. In my opinion, he's vastly underrated when people name legends of the club. The second, a young Scot from Falkirk called Gary Gillespie. A then raw but composed on the ball defender who made 14 appearances and looked a real player in the making.

One man's misfortune is often another's opportunity. This was proven by youngters, Garry Thompson and Andy Blair. Thompson stood in for Fergie and scored nine times to underline his potential while Blair deputised ably for Yorath. Despite now being a very marked man, Wallace netted 15 times. But the side still looked vulnerable at the back and a couple of experienced players short of emulating the previous season.

A lot of attention focused on our new away kit. The Sky Blue "egg timer" design home strip was very popular. For our travels, a chocolate brown version was introduced. Yes, brown not just the colour of chocolate but something rather more unpalatable. Even today the strip regularly crops up in worst kit of all time polls and articles.

The all brown outfit was worn in the away game at West Brom. Maybe the only time the colour of a football kit provided apt comment on a performance as we were stuffed 7-1. In an act of depraved loyalty come self torture, me and my mates stayed to the bitter end of one of my most humiliating experiences I've ever had in a football stadium. Afterwards, we got legged everywhere. The train broke down on the way home too. Suffice to say, I've had better days.

All the same, City finished a respectable 10th in the table. The home clash with Manchester United was a thriller that the Sky Blues edged 4-3. Milne vowed to address the weaknesses but was equally adamant the core of a vibrant youth policy held the key to a bright future.

Having just left school and having my own money in time for the next season, I really looked forward to August 1979. Milne attempted to address the defensive frailties by spending well over half a million, a lot for us, on two back four players. David Jones a full back from Everton and centre half, Gary Collier brought in via Bristol City.

There were a couple of problems with this. Both were instantly jinxed by injury. When they did play they looked way off the pace. A bloke that sat by us nicknamed Jones, "Rhino" in reference to his lack of speed. That cruel term actually being one of the kindest applied to the pair who were both eventually shipped out at a loss after failing to make any sort of first team impact.

Another stunner was the eve of season departure of skipper Yorath to Tottenham. The club had a good offer for a player plagued by injury the previous season. With Andy Blair showing promise it probably made sense. But I didn't see it that way. I was fuming. To me, selling our best players was becoming an all too annoying regular occurrence.

I was in Blackpool on holiday when somebody staying in the same hotel told me we'd sold Yorath. Shocked, I phoned the club from a red telephone box. The brief exchange went something like this.

"Hello, Coventry City Football Club."

"Hello. Is it true we've sold Terry Yorath?"

"Yes, it's true."

"You've got no ambition. I hate you." The poor woman on the other end of the receiver must have thought I was a nutcase. She would have had a fair point.

I managed to go to most away games but we flattered to deceive being very inconsistent. I was just happy to start collecting grounds. Crossing Third Division Ewood Park off the list was a nice FA Cup bonus but I could have done without the 1-0 reverse. We took a good following that day. There were under sixteen turnstiles and blokes in their forties were going through to gain cheaper entry past seemingly helpless bemused home stewards.

The week before, we had beat mighty Liverpool at home with one of the youngest teams the clubs had ever fielded. City had a fine home record in general during that period at a time when the Reds were virtually unassailable. I once saw an interview with Anfield great, Grahame Souness who described Highfield Road as the jinx ground of his career. When Terry Yorath was at City he had some almighty personal battles with Souness. Some of their shuddering tackles were on each other made you wince.

The season became one of transition. The team that had just two years earlier had pushed for Europe was slowly being dismantled. With youngsters you get promise but also frustration. Which is fair enough because it's all part of the education process. But football fans want success yesterday so it's always difficult for lads just breaking into the first team. We slipped into the bottom half and I became more skeptical about our selling habit.

To be honest, when I look back at that time now, I don't like myself. My wanting for City to do well became all consuming. I couldn't see reason, had no time for logic. Going away, you increased your chances of getting a good kicking and I craved reward for risk. I also remember my language being pretty appalling during matches. Odd because I've never been that given to swearing otherwise. But football can turn a person into a different beast altogether.

I attended a City home game recently when we were having a pretty bad day at the office. We went a goal down early on and a couple of guys who were sitting by us started having a go at the players incessantly. In the end, another fan got annoyed and asked, "Why don't you try encouraging the team and stop being so negative?"

One of the blokes went into a loud and prolonged diatribe about how he'd been a season ticket holder for many seasons and had earned the right to say exactly what he felt. I love football or I wouldn't be writing this but I just felt like saying, it isn't that important. Of course it matters but if you've had any kind of life you should learn in context of loved ones, family etc, a football result isn't the end of the world.

Perhaps the game gives us a valve to express emotions that we wouldn't otherwise reveal. An outlet for the pain and pent up restraints we place on ourselves. Hearing that rant reminded me of my own teenage years. When an outcome not in my hands on a Saturday afternoon shaped my mood for the next few days. Until a fresh slate loomed in the shape of the next fixture.

I went to Maine Road early on during the 79-80 season with Lawrence. He'd started travelling to the blue Manc matches with the Rugby branch of the Manchester City supporters club. He invited me to go with them. They were a good bunch who on finding out I was only employed on a government slave training course, just charged me a quid for the coach trip.

Man City were under the flamboyant Malcolm Allison for his ill fated return to the club. He'd spent crazy amounts by the transfer fees criteria of the time. Yet they were struggling badly at the foot of the table. The atmosphere in the pubs before the game was one of cynicism and acerbic comments aimed at club chairman, Peter Swales. They suffered years in the wilderness and the older fanbase certainly paid its suffering dues before the successful transition of the Arab money men turned them into a global force.

We went on their main terrace, The Kippax, on a section Lawrence referred to as Critic's Corner. I soon found out why. I thought I was good at moaning but this lot were different class. That being until an old adage kicked in, "Are your team on a bad run? Then play Coventry." They rattled in three goals without reply. Outside the ground, an old bloke walked round with a sandwich board strapped to him. It said, "The end is nigh." I knew how he felt.

Even top division grounds back then were a long way from the plush concourses that cater for today's punters. The revered pie and Bovril being pretty much standard fare. I once saw a "meal deal" comprising of a bag of crisps, a Wagon Wheel and a carton of Ribena. Hardly eating at The Ritz. Going without a decent dinner or tea was part and parcel of going away. A decent chip shop near an away ground being akin to finding The Holy Grail.

A very laddish mentality persisted in football fan culture. The songs were full of macho chest pumping such as, "City lads, we are here, shag your women and drink your beer." I felt a bit sorry for the females who attended matches back then having to put up with the caveman element.

I also went to Anfield for the first time that season. The Reds around then had one of the best sides I've ever seen and hammered us 4-0. Our coach parked up by a graveyard. On returning from the game to travel home, we sat waiting to depart. From behind each headstone outside the church, little Scouse heads popped up and proceeded to pelt our coach with stones. The kids had planned it like a military operation.

My travels also took me to the other Merseysider's, Everton. I got on the bus delighted on having secured a draw. The smile soon got wiped off my face when I realised I'd boarded the coach of the Coventry branch of the Everton supporters club. Hired out by the same company we went with, it was identical to our transport. I felt like Benny Hill at the end of his show as I was chased back out into the street.

That typified a time when you could get into dodgy situations because of your own innocence. The dark clouds of trouble were treated as occupational hazard. There had to be a good degree of personal bravado or you'd never have seen a game. While some of the things that happened were inexcusable, football supporters had little more in their lives. Jobs were scarce, hope low, fighting a release.

The terraces have always reflected social change as much as street fashion. Away days by train in the late 70's were populated heavily with punks and skinheads. But the majority weren't following trends but becoming tribal because that became the only sense of belonging they had left.

My first decade as a football fan had seen me find affinity in my local team, passed down to me by my Dad. That allegiance was never in doubt. There is nothing I can understand less than not supporting the club closest to where you live or place of birth. This makes the glory, if it comes, as great as the inevitable pain. At times it's more gory hunting than glory but that doesn't mean it's any less worth it.

In those ten years, we never had a sniff of a trophy despite holding on to our place with the elite. It never occurred to me or any of my City supporting friends to jump ship and land on a more successful clubs bandwagon. There's no choice when your team is in your blood.

Love Will Tear Us Apart The Early 80's

"We've sold Ian Wallace."
"You're joking!"
"Its true. It's in the Cov Telegraph."
"It's finished. I'm finished. Everything is finished."
Nothing brings emotional hysteria into football like the selling of a fans favourite. So when Ian Wallace departed in 1980 for Nottingham Forest I was incandescent with rage. Despite us getting one million plus, this brought little consolation as Jimmy Hill said the money raised from the transfer would go towards building a new leisure centre at the Ryton training ground.

Called the Sports Connexion, it would offer the players added facilities and also be open for public membership. Thus dragging the training ground up to date and bringing in constant revenue. Wallace's replacement would be Tommy English, another bright youth system product.

I wasn't buying into it at all. Again, I felt this showed a lack of ambition where it really mattered, on the playing field. Wally had been one of my favourites in Sky Blue despite his goal output dropping year on year. I just failed to see how you could hope to build a decent side when they would ultimately be sold to rivals.

In truth, Wallace without Ferguson was never quite the same. The telepathy they had between them was rare. Without each other their careers never quite touched the same heights. Wallace averaged around a dozen goals in his three full seasons at Forest. When Fergie departed a year later for Everton he would be plagued by niggling injuries for the rest of his career.

Apart, they were like Batman without Robin, one part of a lethal chemistry missing. But in my annoyance, I became again blind to logic. In truth, selling a revered player is a test of faith, but players like all staff move on. The supporters and the club itself are only the constants. New faces come in, old ones depart. You as a fan either accept this and move on with it or ultimately find something else to do on match days.

In defence of the way I felt then, many stout young City fans I knew from that era rarely go now. I'm pretty sure being consistent sellers of star talent is a contributing factor. The problem is, as a fan, you emotionally invest in young players. You accept they will make point costing errors while gaining experience. But as soon as they are anywhere near the real deal, they move elsewhere. A real loyalty tester.

As 1980-81 started there were plenty of youngsters to be patient with and excited about. It is to their great credit that before many months had passed the supporters would enthusing about their raw talent and had stopped talking about Wallace's departure. Things began annoyingly though, with a defeat at Birmingham.

When we got out of the motor and parked up, a few young urchins approached us and said, "Do you want us to look after your car mate? Only a couple of quid." This practice was a early eighties phenomenon. Kids operating an extortion racket. The inference being if you don't give us a couple of pounds, on returning, the car won't be in the condition you left it in. Fine examples of the Thatcherite self starter ethic.

Things picked up with a fine home win against Arsenal. I went to Old Trafford for the first time in the League Cup and saw us triumph by a single goal. I'd always wanted to go there and it meant a lot to win although the competition had two legs in the opening round back then. We won the home tie by the same score as well. City didn't take many to Old T for the first meeting and the United fans taunted us with the, "Did you come in a taxi?" old chestnut.

So that made victory sweeter. I went on my own and worried about the natives being restless in defeat, asked a policeman, "Do you get much trouble here?" Back came the reply, "Only when United lose son. Only when they lose." He'd obviously picked up on my naivety.

Early September brought a incident that remains talked about to this day. We were leading Crystal Palace when, at the opposite end to where I was sitting, Clive Allen rifled a corker in from a fine free kick just outside the box. Begrudgingly I thought, that's a good goal. Except it wasn't. Despite the fact the ball had clearly gone deep into the net, hit the stanchion and bounced back out, one bloke didn't see it like that. Fortunately for us, he was the referee.

There was uproar but the ref remained adamant. No goal. The game was shown on Match of the Day then broadcast on Sunday's. Confirmed to millions. A clear a goal as you will see. But there were no video replays. The referee's word was final. And we'd got out of jail, winning 3-1 to add to Allen and Palace's misery.

The Sky Blues had made an astute signing in the form of Irish midfielder, Gerry Daly. A skilful ball player, he complimented Steve Hunt perfectly, adding some know how to the youthful mix. A long midweek trip down to Brighton in the next round of the League Cup brought a fine 2-1 win Tommy English again scoring and looking promising. Despite his movement being slightly awkward in the eyes of some, he began to form a decent partnership with Garry Thompson as Fergie's injury woes continued.

But the dreaded inconsistent streak again reared its ugly head in the very next game when Everton left Highfield Road 5-0 victors. That became much the pattern of he season with the knockout competitions bringing out the best in what became a close knit squad.

There was a surprise when Tommy Hutchison departed for Man City along with McDonald. The 33 year old became a key signing for John Bond and would go on to famously score at both ends in that season's FA Cup Final. In those last couple of years at Cov, Hutch went even more up in my estimation. His work rate is rarely mentioned but often deployed on the right, he sacrificed his more skilful side of the his game running himself into the ground especially away.

It is to his testament, if you ask fans of a certain vintage their favourite ever City player, the answer will almost certainly be Hutchison. His dribbling prowess lit up some dark days and he never gave less than 100%. In 2002 I won a poetry competition connected with the club. Tommy presented me with my prize at half time during a home game with Norwich. I was awestruck during this proud moment with my boyhood hero.

Next up in the League Cup, came a disappointing one-each draw at home to Cambridge. I stood on their minuscule away end for the replay. Someone joked, "This terrace is so small, we're standing at the front and the back." A tight tussle ended with Hunt scoring the only goal. We were in the last eight, interest building all the time, including media attention focusing on Milne's starlets.

We were drawn at Watford in the quarter finals. The day before the game I came down with a monster of a heavy cold. By the afternoon of the match I'd rarely felt so rough in my life but remained determined to go even if I infected the rest of the coach. Unselfish me. I slept all the way there and felt in a haze as we walked to the stadium.

As kick off approached, hordes of Coventry fans were still trying to gain admission through the hopelessly overwhelmed turnstiles. Many started pushing at a wide double doored metal gate. Whether it was opened or gave way, I'm not sure, but the intended exit swung open becoming a makeshift entrance. As if on a surging tide I was swept inside Vicarage Road by the body weight of others.

A quite frightening incident, when you're no longer in control of your own movement. Commonplace never the less at packed games. It would take tragedy of heartbreaking proportions before anything was done to address the madness. Many City fans went through that gate with ticket stubs intact or without even having a ticket at all.

We managed to find a spot with a half decent view. Under Graham Taylor, Watford were on the ascent. A journey that would take them to great heights. Thompson had a magnificent game that night scoring twice as the sides shared four first half goals. That was the final score. Watching a game when you feel like crap through illness is a strange experience. You want to take it all in but somehow the action passes by in a blur.

Own of my main memories of the early December, Watford home replay day is walking home from the shops with my Mum. She pointed to a newspaper billboard outside the newsagent which pronounced, "Beatle shot dead." I rushed in to buy the paper. While I wasn't a big Fab Four fan it was a stunning somber moment as I read of the killing of John Lennon. It brought home how precious life is and you never know what is coming next, even for a much loved songwriting genius.

The match that night may well have been the finest moment for that young Sky Blue side. They stormed home 5-0 and played some brilliant stuff including a great strike from another promising kid, Peter Bodak. Despite being a tough physical outfit, Watford had no answer. Euphoria swept the ground at the final whistle. For the first time in Coventry's history, they were in a major semi final. With the youngest squad the club had assembled. We were in a winter wonderland that Christmas.

A rare but empathic home win over West Brom followed. Milne's young charges began to pick up regular coverage in the sports pages. I went to a Yuletide game at Stoke. The Victoria Ground impressed me. Proper old school, you could sense the history and it evoked an intimidating atmosphere. Cov came away with a decent 2-2 draw.

My first trip to Elland Road soon followed in the FA Cup 3rd round. We made an early start and the Sky Blues team coach passed us near the motorway turn off. Somebody said, "Let's just follow the coach. It'll lead us to the ground." So we did and the City team bus led us to their hotel, well away from the stadium. Oh, for the invention of the sat nav. We came away with a draw won the replay, then beat Birmingham in the next round. Cup runs must be like buses. You wait years then two come at once.

The home League Cup semi final first leg with West Ham went into City folklore. An awful blunder by our keeper Les Sealey and an own goal from Gary Thompson gifted the Hammers a 2-0 lead. The vibes in the ground were awesome. You could feel the electricity and expectation. There had been pockets of trouble outside the stadium beforehand and now it was all going wrong on the pitch.

But the youthful Sky Blues had other ideas. Thompson had the game of his life, scoring twice at the right end. His winner came two minutes from time after Daly had equalised. I'd never felt so elated at a match before. Steaming back to the social club to watch the highlights I swerved more outbreaks of fighting. Surely we were going to Wembley.

We knew however there would be the most hostile of receptions at Upton Park both on and off the field. I travelled by myself to Euston by train then to the ground via tube. I passed a City fan who had been stabbed in the arm and was bleeding heavily as passers-by ran to help. For the first time at a match, I admit I felt afraid. Surely football wasn't worth this sort of violence.

The game took place in what felt like a cauldron on a bitter cold winter's night. The Sky Blues fought bravely but were never at their best going down 2-0. With the match just two minutes from extra time, Jimmy Neighbour netted to send the East End wild. The dream had been crushed in the cruelest of late twists. Coins flew into the away end, some sharpened. I felt sickened in every way.

On the tube back to Euston some huge Cockney chap started slating City. He raged, "Coventry don't deserve go to Wembley. All they want is to find a couple of decent players and sell them on at profit. They'd take that above winning a trophy any day. Disgraceful." That was the last thing I wanted to hear. I fought the feeling at the back of my mind, I'd just met the truth monster.

I took two days off the work placement I was doing at the time. The supervisor handed me a form to explain my absence. He looked stunned as he read, "I took sick leave because I was recovering from a cup semi final defeat." Needless to say they never offered me a proper job.

The following Saturday, I went to White Hart Lane in the FA Cup 5th round. We were comprehensively beaten by a

Glenn Hoddle inspired Tottenham. In the space of a few days, hopes of that elusive first trip to Wembley had been dashed twice. As a fan, it was hard to pick yourself up so I assume that happened to the players too.

We lost seven out of the next nine. This included a League return to Leeds. I went with my next door neighbour, Charlie. He stood up and I sat down. Leaving the ground after a 3-0 hiding, I managed to get lost, unable to find where our coach was parked. Charlie, having had a few beers, crashed out as soon as he got onboard our bus. So he was unable to tell them I was missing.

By the time I realised where we'd parked, the coach had left for Coventry. I asked a policeman where the train station was, explaining my situation. He said I could go with him and his colleagues in the back of the police wagon and they'd drop me off. So I ended up sitting with a dozen coppers before being let out like an escaping criminal.

I then found I hadn't enough cash for the train. My family didn't have a landline phone in those days. I had to phone directory enquiry's for the number of our local social club. I asked the barmaid to go and tell my Dad to go to Coventry station and pay my fare home from that end which he did.

The train had four changes. I fell asleep on the last leg of the journey and if the guard hadn't woke me up just before the train reached Cov, I'd have travelled on to the next stop. Which was Brighton! I finally got home at three o'clock in the morning. The next day, Charlie said, "I was sozzled. I knew something was missing from that coach." Yes, me! The thought that my away travels were jinxed grew ever stronger.

That paranoia increased when I missed my only game of the season at Middlesbrough and we won. The season that promised so much petered out. All the same I couldn't wait for 1981-82. But before a ball had been kicked, came two massive shocks. Firstly Gordon Milne was moved upstairs to a form of the dreaded director of football type role. This usually means, we haven't the guts and/or the dosh to sack you.

I must admit this pleased me. I thought Milne had taken us as far as he could and had held a personal campaign for his removal even having, Milne Out! badges made. I was badly wrong and owe the bloke an apology. Milne did brilliantly for years with limited resources and our best players being sold from over his head. In retrospect, he was a fine manager but my knee jerk impatient success today self couldn't grasp that.

His replacement was the highly rated and respected, Dave Sexton, previously of big guns Chelsea and Manchester United. Gifted at getting the best out of talented youngsters with a reputation for tactical knowledge, it seemed like a major scoop for the club. I renewed my season ticket with enthusiasm. Then came the second surprise, one not previously experienced by a football supporters of a club in England.

"They're putting in seats all around the ground!"

"You're joking!"

"It's true. It's in the Cov Telegraph. The terraces are over. We're going all seater."

"It will never work. It's finished. I'm finished. Everything is finished."

Jimmy Hill was always a man ahead of his time. Football at the time was and had been haunted for years by the curse of hooliganism. Hill sought to open the game back up to families and those put off by continual aggro in and outside of grounds.

One such person being my Dad. He witnessed some very unsavoury incidents and stopped attending matches. I persuaded him to go on the Kop at Highfield Road where there was rarely any trouble against Norwich who we rarely had any trouble with. And yep, where he stood, a load of fighting broke out with Norwich fans in the wrong end.

Hill's vision meant seats for all. A clearer view, a friendlier vibe, became his means of selling the idea to fans who were mainly, highly skeptical. A lot of the seating from the revamped terraces were out in the open. Now it's one thing watching say, American Football in an uncovered environment on a hot sunny day but quite another watching our version of football when it's caning down with rain.

Me and Ray sneaked into Highfield Road during the stadium remodel and our initial reaction was one of horror. They were changing a good traditional ground and making it a thing of experiment. Hill remained unrepentant. All seater stadiums represented the future, he argued. And he was right as usual. But by the time the future arrived, protection from the elements was considered a prerequisite.

The new era started at HR as brightly as could be possible. A 2-1 win over Manchester United on a lovely late August day. A new bright youngster on the block by the name of Steve Whitton scored twice. Muscular and powerful, Whitton offered something different and defences were baffled by a player with deceptive ball skills in addition to his prowess.

The next home date saw Jimmy Hill's idea of a trouble free totally seated ground dashed. City comprehensively thrashed Leeds 4-0. Away fans were now housed in one section of the Sky Blue Stand. Segregation being delivered by rows of unused empty seats manned by stewards and a few policemen. With events going horribly wrong on the pitch for the Yorkshire-men, some of their fans decided to disgrace themselves off the field.

They began ripping out seats and throwing them, down at Coventry fans then at the police as they attempted to quell the disturbance. The very essence of Hill's trouble free manifesto were being used as weapons to harm both ordinary supporters and officers of the law. It had became clear if a section of the crowd want to create problems, it would take more than enforced seating to stop this occurring.

Sexton's new regime had a shuttering start. Just five wins gained by the start of December, all at home. Hopes of another League Cup run were dashed. City went to Everton for a first leg tie with their manager, Howard Kendall under severe pressure. Rumour had it if the game was lost, he'd would be gone. The Toffeemen had a recent signing in their ranks, one Mick Ferguson. The law of the old boy applied in both legs. Kendall being saved, to lead his team to later considerable glory.

Under Sexton, City were playing the neat tidy passing football associated with the coach. But they lacked the cutting edge to capitalise on periods of possession. The squad was too light on numbers. Good results as ever were quickly followed by bad. Attendances meanwhile were falling further with supporters showing little sign of buying into Hill's brave new world.

There were some good moments. We drew Man City in the FA Cup fourth round. Me and Steve Collins went with Lawrence and the Citizen's Rugby mob. They took us in their social club for a pre match drink. There were some other Coventry fans in there too. Suddenly an almighty fracas occurred with some home fans unhappy about the presence of the away contingent in their club. It reached a flashpoint as fists flew everywhere.

City played superbly that day and ran out deservedly 3-1 victors. Peter Bodak topped things off with a wonder goal, running over half the length of the pitch before audaciously chipping big Joe Corrigan. The silence of the Manc supporters we'd travelled with was a delight on the journey home. The game featured on Match of the Day with Bodak's strike lauded nationally.

Bodak proved to be one of the most enigmatic players I've seen. Supremely self confident to the point of cockiness, he produced the odd flash of genius like at Maine Road. But he could also be mind numbingly mediocre. Bodak went on to play for both Manchester clubs without tearing up any trees though in fairness, did have injury woes.

We progressed to the quarter finals. Played on my 19th birthday, away to West Brom. Cyrille Regis wrecked my party with a devastating solo run and clinical finish. To the credit of Sexton and his new charges, they only lost three more times that season, including a 6-1 routing of Sunderland at home. I also finally tasted success at The Hawthorns.

But my phobia of being blighted by a travelling curse gathered pace when I missed a rare away game at Southampton. The outcome, a 5-5 draw with many City fans saying it was the greatest game of football they'd ever witnessed. I felt gutted. For the last away game of the season, we went up to the blue half of Manchester again. To our delight, history repeated itself and we won 3-1 again. This time though, me and Steve Collins were lucky to live to tell the tell.

For some mad reason we sat in the home end, behind the goal. When Steve Whitton scored, we instinctively jumped up and went ballistic. A few Manc's gathered round us fuming. We just about avoided as a slap as one of them diplomatically said, "You jump up again and you're both dead." So we had to show restraint as Whitton went on to net a hat trick. We legged it out the ground. A great win but the feeling we were taking our life in our hands just for football started to leave a nasty taste.

On the perennial tight budget, Sexton appeared to have laid down decent foundations. He made a clever move by bringing in former England captain, Gerry Francis. Though never the same player after a succession of bad injuries, Francis proved a good on-field mentor for the kids. They had the legs and he provided the experience.

So once again we looked forward to a new season with excitement. But sadly for us and Sexton, 82-83 proved a disappointment. We started in average fashion, enjoying a fine purple patch in mid season. My New Years Day hangover eased with a good win at Luton. City were comfortable in the top half, even talking of Europe. Few could have expected what followed.

Just two more league wins were gained during the rest of the season. We just about stayed up. Somehow, shoddily, nearly every player on the books had their contracts coming up for renewal at the same time, the close season. During the last months of 82-83, Coventry made no real attempt to entice its promising youngsters to stay. Whether this affected morale and ultimately results is debatable.

For me, Sexton was disgracefully let down by the board. He didn't help himself in that he clearly didn't rate or had issues with Gerry Daly who he let rot in the reserves. But that happens in football. Sexton given raw material, never had the backing, money or otherwise to be given a fair crack of producing something tangible. He departed like the vast majority of the squad in a summer bloodletting of epic proportions.

All this became disillusioning to me. Bereft of players due to shambolic planning in the boardroom, riding our luck in the trouble stakes when we went away, football didn't seem like fun any more. But the game isn't the most popular in the world for no reason. It's ability to hurt, thrill, madden, is never ending. A beautiful mass of contradictions.

That Joke Isn't Funny Anymore The Mid 80's

For the 1983-84 season, I decided not to renew my season ticket and knock going away on the head for a while. I'd still attend home matches. The reasons were as much fiscal as football. I'd been on the dole for a fair old time now. Footie ate up most of my spare money. At this time I'd started going out drinking and was also in the process of forming a band, my other love being music.

There were football considerations too. I felt hurt and betrayed when that young side was sold off. Having gone home and away, I invested much time and money in following a bunch of lads who would now realise their potential elsewhere. The case of Garry Gillespie particularly got to me. He always looked like a top player in the making although being young, had errors in him. Sexton helped polish and nurture his talent. He was now the finished article and gone.

The new manager charged with the mother of all rebuilding jobs was announced as former Sky Blue playing legend, Bobby Gould. Coventry born and bred. Bobby had a major hand in the club's rise to the top flight, firing in a rake of goals for Jimmy Hill. He went on have something of a travelling nomad of a career before entering management at Bristol Rovers where he did well.

Now his job was to add to the few players left, build a decent squad in a few months on a limited budget and keep us up, minimum. Not a big ask! He set about the task with gusto, recruiting non stop. Some, the fans had heard of, like hard man defender Sam Alladyce and Tottenham fringe striker, Terry Gibson. But there were a lot of unknowns, forward Dave Bamber, midfielder Micky Gynn, full back

Stuart Pearce and a plethora of others. Someone remarked not so much a who's who but who?

But fair play to Gould who used his expert knowledge of the lower divisions and non league to bring in players he thought were good and hungry enough to succeed at England's highest level. There was a whiff of the transfers in bring akin to throwing objects at a wall and seeing what sticks. But Gould had little choice. And the passion he had for the club was immense and undeniable.

Terry Gibson epitomised what Bobby Gould wanted from his players. Freed from the role of back up at Spurs, given his chance at last, the diminutive but razor sharp frontman soon became a terrace, sorry, all seater hero. 11 points were gathered from the first 5 games. The team though strangers were galvanised by Gould evoking a determination to prove people wrong. They think you're not good enough, you show them. Similar to his own playing career.

The decent start included a home victory over Midlands rivals, Leicester and a fine win at Arsenal. Dave Bamber stunned Highbury with the only goal. Me and Ray went to a League Cup tie at Highfield Road with Grimsby. They brought a large feisty following and scraps broke out in pubs surrounding the ground. The grip of the hooligan showed no sign of abating.

On October 1st 1983, Ray got married. The reception was held at The Lunchbox about ten minutes from Highfield Road. The Sky Blues were at home to Ipswich. I sat with Stephen Gardner watching the speeches and toasts. I said,

"The Cov game kicks off soon. Would we be really bad friends if we left now and went up the match?"

"We would." Said Stephen.

"Shall we go up the match?"

"Yes."

So we made our excuses halfway through the ceremonies and shot off to the game. During the first half as we sat on the now seated open end Kop, it poured down on us. Our carnations drooping, our suits soaked, we watched as City lost. Our karma delivered.

Shortly after, I went with Ray to a home match against Sunderland again sitting in the Kop. Just after half time the was another torrential downpour. The club stewards ushered everyone out of the end into the covered parts of the ground. A good gesture but a fatal flaw with the all seating arrangement again exposed.

Shortly before Christmas, City absolutely caned all conquering Liverpool by four goals to nil. Gibson nettled a hat trick in a perfect display shown on Match of the Day. Gould's side were defying the gloom and doom merchants in style. I'd reneged on my no away games vow a few times, buoyed by the promise of the new era.

A couple of days after Crimbo, I went with Stephen and his Dad to Nottingham Forest. I choose to go with them despite being invited on a mini bus trip to the City Ground with my mates from the Bulls Head pub. A wise choice as those lads got jumped outside a boozer and fought back. Several of them were arrested after the brawl. I remember them getting quite astonishingly high fines at the time compared to punishments dished out for other transgressions in society.

As February began, only a calamitous bad run could see us in relegation trouble. So naturally just 2 points were taken from the next 11 games. Two wins steadied the ship. But then in the next three losing away games, City shipped an astounding seventeen goals. Teenage rookie goalkeeper Perry Suckling being desperately exposed. After all the promise we needed to win the final home game against Norwich to stay up.

Gould had one more ace up his sleeve. He had loaned a striker from Birmingham quite familiar with Highfield Road relegation battles. One, Mick Ferguson. Fergie scored as City clung successfully to a precious 2-1 lead and were safe. Jubilant and relieved supporters flooded the pitch as Gould led the celebrations from the Main Stand.

"We shouldn't be celebrating narrowly avoiding failure." Commented Stephen. Too right. Given the farce Gould inherited perhaps this was an achievement in itself. But the best case scenario being mediocrity, survival being treated like a trophy win, surely had to be reversed if the club were to move on.

Gould decided to bring in a new goalkeeper during close season. He raided Shrewsbury for their number one, Steve Ogrizovic. Forever known as Oggy to affectionate fans and people like me who struggle to spell. Understudy to Ray Clemence, he was a colossal commanding figure with agility to boot. Oggy needed all these attributes as City's first eight matches of 1984-85 brought just one win. That being against Leicester, a match held up for over ten minutes when fighting between the two local rivals fans spilled onto the pitch.

I added Fellows Park to my list of away grounds where we beat Walsall 2-1 in a League Cup first leg. Me and Ray were in our local pub before the second leg, drinking for England. We decided not to go to the game and finish off getting drunk. After all, we were going into a home fixture one up against a club from Division 3. We lost three-nil. A fine example of why you never take anything for granted in football.

For the Highfield Road league clash with Arsenal, myself and Ray hatched up another gem of an idea. We'd go in the away end. I've no idea why. So we paid our money and joined the Gunners contingent in the visitor's enclosure Suddenly, the truth dawned this was completely insane. Why it took us until being surrounded by a couple of thousand North Londoners to realise this, I'll never know. So we told the stewards, we were in fact Coventry fans from Worcester who hadn't been to see City for a good few years and thought we were going in the home end.

Surprisingly they believed us and we were escorted out of the away section towards the West End. Cheers broke out at what they perceived as two rock hard nut-cases having the bottle to go in with the Arsenal mob. We were happy to let them continue in this misconception.

On the Monday, the new managing director of the place where I now worked said to me, "I saw you on Saturday being led out of the away end up the City." He must have thought he was employing some headbanger from a deluded two man firm.

The team were crying out for more attacking flair and goals. Gould strove to address this by bringing in two English players who had been stars of late seventies and early eighties football. He recruited Peter Barnes who made a name for himself with speedy skilful wing play at Manchester City. The second signing was something of a coup for the club.

Cyrille Regis had come to prominence starring for Ron Atkinson's West Brom side putting in some swashbuckling attacking performances laced with plenty of goals. As part of the, "Three Degrees' with Brendon Batson and Laurie Cunningham, he pioneered the breakthrough of black players in football. Racism was commonplace in stadiums in those days. Regis through his sheer footballing talent made bigotry look as stupid as it was.

After Big Ron left, Regis lost his way a bit at Albion. He'd been linked with the biggest clubs in football many times, so him joining Coventry still surprised many. But both he and Barnes looked like they they were going to need time to settle, something Barnes never really did. The preferred direct style of Gould later labelled as route one never suited Regis. Although a big unit, Cyrille did his best work with ball to feet, embracing pass and move tactics.

Results hardly improved. At Christmas time the Sky Blues board delivered Gould the present of being sacked. A passionate man who inherited a farce of others making. You had to feel for Coventry kid, Bobby. But football has no sentiment and he was replaced by his number two, the little known, Don Mackay.

Three wins in a row soon followed. The kind of form surge that often goes hand in hand with managerial change. This must have axed bosses tearing their hair out. I went to Manchester United with Charlie for a FA Cup tie and thankfully came back on the coach with him this time. The only disappointment being the game was lost.

Form went back to being very indifferent. Having a few games left to play, Houdini survival experts, Coventry were handed a mission that looked impossible even by their standards. They'd have to win the last three matches to stay up.

Part one ticked the box, a 1-0 win at Stoke. A group of us stood in the Bulls Head pub car park listening to the game on a car radio. I've always found listening to football on the wireless more nerve wracking than being there live. This proved a prime example. Finally we were able to run into the bar to order a triumphant pint on the back of another single goal victory. A few more followed after a nervy solitary goal triumph at home to Luton.

So to the final fixture, on a sunny Sunday against newly crowned champions, Everton. And that was key. The men from Goodison performed like they had been partying for days. A couple of Coventry players were quoted as saying they could smell alcohol on the breath on some of their opponents. City meanwhile were fighting for their lives. It seemed like watching role reversal. The Sky Blues looked like the table toppers strolling home, 4-1. The last day safety specialists had survived again.

That the lovely day suddenly turned nasty on the way home, clouding over then bursting into a near monsoon, ensuring a good soaking, mattered not. The weather has no effect when you're celebrating yet another great escape. It's a funny feeling though, raising a glass to last gasp staying up yet again.

After the initial sense of ecstasy, a kind of feeling of hollowness, then almost anger, takes over. That you can't go like this. It will catch up with you in the end if you continually flirt with destiny. So the pub that night wasn't full of jubilation but more a longing to end the tag of being last day drama merchants. Mind you, I still had an hangover fit for an Everton player the next day.

Don Mackay stayed in charge for 85-86 and the same problems remained. Uninspiring football which still failed to play to the strengths of Regis. The goals of Terry Gibson were again key to our hopes. 11 goals by January in a struggling side is invaluable. So best sell him, that's the Coventry way. Though when Manchester United comes calling it undoubtedly unsettles a player. So inevitably Gibbo departed for Old Trafford.

This season was one that holds few memories for me. The club's squad contained a lot of decent professionals but something was missing. The club seemed stuck in a conundrum with no easy solution. Selling to survive but struggling to do so because they were continually selling. One short term solution became the recruitment of seasoned talent that had passed its best. Mind still sharp but legs not what they were.

Two examples were Kenny Hibbert and Alan Brazil. Both players I'd admired greatly in their pomp at Wolves and Ipswich respectively. But it never really happened in Sky Blue. Brazil in particular disappointed, looking like he'd had not just one too many but three or four. I'm referring to injuries of course.

I went to Oxford to watch us lose and was jealous of the massive investment they'd had. The then only rumours concerning the shady nature of Robert Maxwell didn't alter that. Football fans don't really worry about moral of ethical concerns of where the money is coming from to buy players. There were a few highlights. A thrilling 4-4 draw with Birmingham, a good win at Tottenham. But another impending brush with last gasp safety shone like a display of neon lights. After a thrashing at Liverpool, Mackay quit with just three games left and our First Division future again in the balance. Club stalwarts from the Jimmy Hill era took over for a seemingly attempt at a short term fix. George Curtis and John Sillett bled Sky Blue.

A win at home to Luton was followed by defeat at West Ham. Highfield Road victory over QPR signalled time for the familiar wipe of relieved sweaty brows. Even so, many were surprised when the duo were appointed as a full time permanent management team. They were clearly popular with the players but had no experience of high level management. It was a gamble the board thought worth taking.

The key thing is in football, you never know just what is around the corner. Things can change quickly and dramatically without warning, as Coventry fans were about to find out. The ethos instilled in Curtis and Sillett during Coventry's remarkable rise to the top in the 1960's may have belonged to a different era. But good values are perennial. And without warning, the Sky Blues were about to embark on an adventure without parallel that would end with even Jimmy Hill barely able to contain tears of joy.

True Faith 1986-1987

"While we sing together, we will never lose."

The key words of the Sky Blue song penned in the Jimmy Hill era, one of unprecedented success for the club. It was as if during the summer of 1986, John Sillett and George Curtis used the mantra as a template. The playing staff showed only a few changes.

Having inherited a group of solid seemingly unspectacular professionals, the new management duo set about playing to their strengths, building an unshakable team spirit. A sense of unity, a siege mentality of a squad written off. That they could prove the doubters wrong, almost like, while we stick together, we will never lose.

The playing to individual's strong points was most noticeable in a revitalised Cyrille Regis. The ball now played predominately accurately to his feet or chest, in more advanced positions. He looked like a new major signing. You could see the self belief flooding back in Regis because at last he was being coached by people who prioritised his strongpoints.

Regis now had further help upfront with the addition of Keith Houchen. Eyebrows were raised when he moved three divisions up the league's despite a short but ill fated spell at Scunthorpe. Previously, Houchen had made his name scoring frequently for Hartlepool. However, he became best known for cooling slotting home a penalty for York City that sensationally knocked Arsenal out of the FA Cup. Cup upsets against a North London team, now there's an idea.

From the outset it was clear he was unlikely to be a prolific scorer for City. But what Houchen did provide was a unyielding willingness, a work rate that provided the legs to allow Cyrille to concentrate on his finer assets. Plus, both coaches being resolute gritty defenders in their playing days, they utilised this knowledge to the full. Suddenly, Coventry were a difficult to break down, hard to beat unit. A fact reflected when after an opening day reverse at West Ham, Coventry suffered only two losses up to the close of October.

One of these defeats came at Oxford, where I was searched by a policeman on entering the ground.

"Have you been drinking?" He asked as I stumbled while stopping to be frisked.

"No, I'm on drugs." I joked. It took me about five minutes to convince the humourless member of the constabulary I was jesting before he finally let me pass. On the pitch, the team were a picture of steadiness. Oggy as ever impeccable in goal while Trevor Peake and Brian Kilcline formed a central defensive partnership that proved difficult for Division One strikers to breach. The gritty Lloyd McGarth did the dirty work in midfield. While on the wing, Dave Bennett began to rediscover the form that had made him such an exciting prospect at Manchester City.

A thrilling 4-3 festive win over Tottenham at Highfield Road encapsulated the new feeling of optimism that flooded through players and fans. Of course, we'd been here before, experiencing spectacular second half season collapses but something seemed different this time.

In those days you'd often see footballers out drinking. The City players could often be spotted in pubs, looking like a bunch of mates bonding together. In these days of intense media scrutiny this would probably be impossible. Then, you just thought fair play. It heightened the feeling the squad were united as one.

So a rare sense of optimism greeted a FA Cup fourth round tie at Old Trafford as I boarded a train packed like a sardine tin. The Cup campaign had kicked off with a low key but convincing home win over Bolton, most notable for a rare goal by City left back, Greg Downs. A balding cult figure, Downs epitomised what the new management team were about. Non stop commitment for the cause. United had a new manager in Alex Ferguson, faced with the task of turning round their ailing fortunes in the Liverpool dominated decade.

We kept in good spirits despite having to stand in the train corridor all the way to Manchester. Houchen gave us the lead and we always looked compact and comfortable. One goal proved enough although I hear that Fergie fellow did a fairly decent job for the Reds after that.

A good day despite again being forced to stand on the train for the whole return journey. In the pub that night, I drunkenly declared, "We'll win the Cup. Our name is on it. It's our year." I'm not sure if I really believed it or the beer was sounding off but you did sense something in the air.

Another away tie at Stoke brought another single goal win courtesy of Micheal Gynn. Despite being on the small side, Gynn had real speed and a low centre of gravity that troubled defences as he ran at them. I can't recall much about that game because despite being over six foot tall I barely saw a thing on the packed Victoria Ground away terraced end. There was a lot of swaying bodies, moments where control of your movement became determined by others. I hated those situations in congested stadiums and was just glad to leave unscathed and victorious.

We stood on the train there and back by the toilets. There was a rumour some trains had carriages with seats in but we were seeing little evidence to support this. So I happily accepted the offer of a lift by car from my mate Dave Lanchbury for the last eight tie at Sheffield Wednesday. Lanch followed City to every home and away game and had an encyclopaedic knowledge of the best pubs to drink at on away trips. A truly vital asset.

At the time I worked at a factory called Sandvik. In those days the Cup draw would take place on a Monday dinner time broadcast on radio only. We'd all gather round a small transistor in the rest room. While disappointed at another away tie, the general feeling was a trip to Hillsborough represented a chance for further progress, to our first ever FA Cup semi final.

Lanch duly delivered the business on the decent away boozer front and we settled for a place at the side of the pitch once inside the ground. The behind the goal end allocated to us, Leppings Lane was rammed. Though never in your wildest nightmares would you have thought such a scenario would lead to such horrific tragedy just two years later.

The match brought one of the finest away performances I'd seen City produce. Regis and Houchen had too much for Wednesday and we ran out worthy 3-1 victors. That night in the pub everybody said this was our year and it definitely wasn't just beer talk. Something special was taking place. In the league we remained in the top half, in the Cup we marched on, happy days.

A cheer went up in the rest room when we drew Leeds United, 70's giants now residing in the Second Division. The semi finals in those days were played at neutral grounds. Rightly so in my view, rather than the modern money grabbing, Cup Final devaluing exercise of last four ties taking place at Wembley. As Spring approached a sense of expectation prevailed in the City like I'd never experienced before.

It must have been hard for the players to concentrate in the league particularly at home but they kept on delivering favourable form. One evening home game against Oxford, we got up to the top of the steps on the Kop and could barely progress further. The club were employing a system where you needed ticket stubs from home league games to ensure Semi Final tickets. This led to increased gates as desired but the Kop was so dangerously packed against Oxford that night we gave up trying to see and went to the Mercers Arms pub over the road.

The Kop had become fully all standing once again in 1985. That end represented the most failed aspect of Hill's premature future vision. Exposed to the winter with viewing not the best it reduced many's favourite part of the ground, warts and all, to a pretty rotten place to watch a match. Thankfully, the board took the fan's concerns into consideration and the stadium was no longer fully kitted out with seats. Thus allowing customer choice, vital to any business.

But on occasions like the Oxford match you saw where Hill was coming from. I felt like the ultimate bandwagon merchant leaving the ground early. But we got to the top of the steps leading up to the Kop and just couldn't get any further. Tempers were flaring. I always preferred the terraces for the more mundane run of the mill matches where you had room to manoeuvre.

I returned to Hillsborough via coach trip from The Humber Pub. Full of old school nutters who had as one bloke put it, "Supported the club through thick and fights." The game itself was a tremendous tussle. Leeds, I have to admit, looked for long periods like the higher division side. The

Yorkshire-men took the lead in the 14th minute through David Rennie and it stayed that way for over an hour until Gynn and Houchen dramatically turned it right round in our favour.

But a late Dave Edwards equaliser meant extra time. You could see Sillett and Curtis on the pitch galvanising the players, demanding one last push. Dave Bennett carved his name into club folklore with the goal that put City in front. Despite some tense moments it remained that way. A milestone had been removed from around her necks. No longer would opposition fans taunt us with, "You've never been to Wembley!" We were there.

It's probably my best moment as a Coventry fan, more so than even the Final. The sense of euphoria that something you had longed for has finally been achieved makes all the other stuff inconsequential. The trudging walks home after defeats, the, "I'm not going again." vow. It all suddenly becomes worth it. In those days, pre Premiership/Sky, reaching the FA Cup Final was the pinnacle for fan and players alike. So the fist pumping hand shaking high fives walk back to the coach was the realisation of a dream come true.

As a kid, I loved Cup Final day on telly. The build up, the colours, humorous banners in the crowd, the band before the game. A truly unique British spectacle. There was always a tinge of envy inside me as the two teams emerged from the tunnel to a huge roar. Now it would be us, playing Tottenham at the home of football.

The atmosphere built and built in Godiva's City. Nearly every car had a Sky Blue ribbon tied to it. Many houses were decorated on the outside in the club's colours. I just had to get my ticket now. I had stubs for the required games so was confident. The closing fixtures saw us lose at Luton immediately after the Leeds game then finish the remaining eight matches undefeated to finish a credible tenth. A fine turnaround after the struggles of previous seasons.

In the last league match before the Final, at home to Southampton, stylish right back Brian Borrows picked up a serious injury that ruled him out of Wembley. A hush descended on the ground as he was carried off. It seemed so unfair on a player who had been pivotal to our revival. And out of keeping with a game played in send-off mode, an almost testimonial vibe.

On the Monday afternoon before the Final, I was playing snooker in town with Ray's brother, Brian Gower. Somebody came into the hall and said the tickets for people with stubs had gone on sale early. There were people camping outside Highfield Road overnight to ensure they were at the front of the queue. We rushed home to get our stubs, legged it up to the stadium only to find tickets were sold out just before we reached the front of the queue. Heartbreak.

The club justified the decision, saying the police forced their hand on safety grounds, there were too many people camped outside. Whatever, this caused a lot of animosity and anger. Which always happens when supply can't meet demand. I walked round in a daze gutted. The biggest occasion in our history and I'd miss out.

Then the night before the final, I was rehearsing upstairs at the Bulls Head pub for the debut gig there of a band I'd formed together with a few mates including Ray. A lad I knew called John Leon came up to me and said there was a strong possibility he could get me a ticket. Somebody was selling. Mark up price of course but so what? He told me if I got round his house first thing, I should be sorted.

That sunny May Saturday morning I felt like Charlie pulling out his golden ticket from the chocolate bar that meant his visit was secured to Willy Wonka's magical factory. I also felt bad for Ray, Brian and others who missed out but simply had to grab the opportunity of a lifetime.

Dressed all in black, I made my way to the train station. Yes, dressed all in black. At the time, I was going through my, The Cure, goth stage. Always dark clad I hadn't sported Sky Blue once in the Cup run. It became a kind of superstition. My mates burst into laughter when they saw me. Covered in Sky Blue, they greeted my appearance with disbelief.

Funnily enough, outside Wembley, a girl somewhat perplexed by my dress code, draped a City scarf over my shoulders and disappeared. I went into flap mode. This went against my lucky mythology. But if I discarded the club's colours that would surely bring bad luck. So in the end, I kept the scarf on and fitted in a bit more with Cup Final day normality.

The train on the way down had buzzed with anticipation and at last, I got a seat. We couldn't get in a pub though and sat on a green drinking cans from an off licence. An open top bus in the distance approached, fans cheering and waving. Thinking they were City, we stood up and applauded. When it got nearer, we realised those on board were Spurs supporters who promptly showered us with cans and coins. No eighties's football event was complete without a bit of the obligatory hassle.

It took an age to get in the ground and I lost my friends. The biggest game of my life and I'd watch it like Billy No Mates. Oh for the mobile phone. On the train to London, some lad had predicted with typical Cov pessimism, "We will lose about six nil, I know it. Spurs will score early. Then it'll be the ultimate nightmare. A nation watching as we get humiliated." The doom merchant's words haunted me as Clive Allen continued his golden goal spree season putting Spurs into an early lead.

City fans tried to raise the players. They responded and Bennett equalised. The game was like a blur, flying by at pace. I attempted to take it all in but it was too much. When I watched the game back on video there were whole chunks I couldn't remember. Unfortunately, Gary Mabbutt scored right in front of me to put Spurs in front. I also will never forget skipper Kilcline going in for a crunching tackle and coming off worse, being helped off, distraught.

Luckily enough, I was bang in line with Houchen's legendary diving header that levelled things up. There hadn't been many better Wembley goals. My feeling was total now. To hell with superstition, we were dealing in destiny. Conformation came when Mabbutt heavily deflected Lloyd's cross into his own net. I looked around at the incredible scenes. A sea of Sky Blue, songs ringing out.

The final whistle and I'm living out my young boyhood dream. John and George dancing, Killer Kilcline lifting the prize. Tears of joy abounding. Amazing then that the train home was stone quiet. Like everyone had given their all off the pitch too, emotions were drained.

That soon changed back in Coventry when the mother of all celebrations commenced. Pubs ran out of draught beer. Jubilant returning fans jumped in fountains, climbed Lady Godiva's famous statue. Parties went on until the early hours of the morning and beyond.

The following day, tens of thousands of people lined the streets for the homecoming. I stood by the Walsgrave pub for necessary liquid refreshments. We waited ages for the open top bus. Until I could wait for the toilet no more. The moment I undid my zip in the gents, a great roar went up.

The bus arrived and drove past just as I relieved myself. Typical.

"They've gone now. You've missed it. That was fantastic." My bladder and I were no longer friends. Walking home, I said to a mate, "I bet that's it. As good as it gets or is ever going to get."

"No wonder you always wear black." He retorted. The problem was the coming years seemed intent on proving me right,

Born Of Frustration 1988-92

There is a school of thought or myth generally perpetuated by the influence of Sky Television and the money it brought into the game, that football didn't start until 1992. That being the year the Premier League began. Everything that came before that was somehow like the Old Testament in The Bible. All pre Messiah, the saviour that became the revamped top flight. Thus the proceeding years are written off as of little importance.

We do often see clips of Wimbledon upsetting Liverpool in the 1988 FA Cup Final, the year after Coventry won it. The message is clear from that footage. Those cheeky upstarts, how dare they upset the status quo, not know their place in the pecking order. It heightened the grievances of the "big club's" who felt they did not get the majority of the television money when they were the club's shown most often.

To them, the equal distribution of TV cash was in fact a disparity. It robbed them of their self assumed God given right to greater fiscal reward. Their history and greater supporter numbers, bigger viewing figures were all put up as evidence. The so called big five clubs of that time felt they deserved a larger slice of the pie.

By 1988, The Premier League was merely thunder rumbling in the distance. Basking in the success of Wembley glory and the financial boost it brought, Coventry's John Sillett boasted, "We will shopping at Harrod's from now on."

The summer's major signing, David Speedie was more of a rough diamond than the jewellery usually found in London's most famous shop. But he was the ultimate competitor, scored regular, valuable goals and for my money had the most underrated passing ability that I've seen in a Sky Blue shirt. Speedie also had one of the most combustible temperaments I've witnessed as well, having numerous run in's with officialdom.

Our Wembley triumph meant we returned there for the Charity Shield where we lost in an uneventful game to Everton. Then the opening day of the 1987-88 league season brought a tasty rematch against Spurs at Highfield Road. We were again the nemesis of the North Londoners winning 2-1.

George Curtis had moved to the more upstairs role of managing director leaving Sillett in sole charge of first team affairs. He adapted admirably and the side looked as comfortable in its skin as the season before. Despite being unable to replicate the Cup success the Sky Blues again finished tenth. Regis top scored with a modest twelve goals but the struggles that had plagued the club looked light years away.

If you look at Sillett's record during his four full seasons at the helm, it reads, 10th, 10th, 7th, 12th. A commendable return that represents the most stable period in the club's otherwise mostly turbulent thirty-four year Division One history. They played neat tidy football on the deck and took a fair bit of beating. This was somewhat under appreciated by the board and some fans alike who thought the Cup triumph would open the door to more silverware.

English clubs had been kicked out of Europe so City were denied this in 1987 and possibly with the seventh position finish two years later. Sadly that season is overshadowed by one of the biggest upsets in FA Cup history when the Sky Blues went to non league Sutton United and lost 2-1. The home side's goals have been played endless times over the years in Cup shock segments. To the extent, not a year goes by when in early January, I don't reach for the remote control to turn over as nightmare of Gander Green Lane is shown yet again.

I have the feeling that if I'm lucky enough to go to heaven, the angel on the pearly gates will look at her clipboard and say, "You come from Coventry? Didn't you get knocked out of the Cup at Sutton in 1989?"

I'd been rehearsing during the game for a gig that night with the band. We walked into the bar just as the result came up on telly. A cheer went up from some of the punters so at first I thought City had won. Then the horrible truth dawned. We'd lost and some bitter sods revelled in the news that the club from the place where they lived had been humiliated. Well sad people.

It blighted an otherwise really decent season. Speedie top scored despite sometimes being deployed in midfield. He performed better there in my opinion though flashes of temper led to constant bother with officials. But I feel every team needs a player like that, to whom losing is unthinkable. If you look at any decent side, there is always that on the edge talisman figure that demands the best out of himself and his teammates, accepting no less.

One way Sillett didn't help himself was with the big money signing of Kevin Drinkell in 1989. Brought in from Glasgow Rangers, he had a disastrous time at City scoring just 5 times in 41 outings. It's worth reading his autobiography for his side of that sorry story but he looked miles off the pace required at England's top level.

Another black mark on Sillett's CV was a second dismal Cup shock exit at Northampton on 8th January 1990. To many fans, the result was more shocking than Sutton due to a dire performance that bordered on casual acceptance of the situation.

The team were still the nucleus of the Wembley triumph. The directors never really backed Sillett with the money required to push on. Despite this, 1989-90 brought twelfth place, and nearly a return to the twin towers in the League Cup. A fine run, featuring a 5-0 thumping of Sunderland in a home quarter final replay, although no doubt Jimmy Hill fixed that in some way. This brought a two leg semi against Brian Clough's Nottingham Forest.

The away encounter came first and a tight terse contest ended in narrow 2-1 defeat. The home leg, a similar hotly contested affair of few chances ended goalless so we just fell short. Both games were played on pitches battered by winter. When you see the immaculate playing surfaces of today and players being rested through tiredness, it makes you wonder how they'd have coped with the mud heaps of yesteryear.

Despite a credible finish of twelfth, some supporters were becoming worried by the lack of goals, the ability to turn draws into victories. Sillett, a former youth coach, was blooding fledging talent such as Steve Livingstone and David Smith. However with whispers of impending league fiscal upheaval in the air, directors across the land were getting jittery.

The question being asked was, had Sillett taken City as far as he could? Maybe this was the wrong question and should have been, would we have kicked on with more investment on players? Speedie top scoring with nine goals said a lot although the acquisition of Scottish striker Kevin Gallacher looked promising.

1989 however was a year that would forever be tainted in football history and far beyond. Ninety six Liverpool supporters lost their lives at Hillsborough. I was on a weekend break in Llandudno that Saturday. You remember where you were when the news broke, watching those horrific pictures being transmitted on television. In the hotel bar, I sat feeling sickened and helpless. Four years earlier there had been a catastrophic fire at Bradford when 65 people perished.

I didn't know at the time but my cousin, David Jowett, a Liverpool fan, attended the Hillsborough semi final and ended up on the pitch helping other fans using advertising hoardings as makeshift stretchers in a desperate situation. He still suffers from trauma to this day. Like so many others, life changed forever during what was supposed to be a pleasurable day out.

Going to a football match and never coming home. It resonated with every fan of every club. Attitudes had to change. But sadly and disgracefully the upper echelons of football clubs, governing bodies of football and society, the police, were too slow to react. Stadiums built for the needs of a bygone time were allowed to become decrepit and dangerous. Mirrored pretty much by the backward complacent thinking of authority.

By the time the 1990 World Cup took place in Italy the overwhelming consensus was that of the need for change. English football fans tainted by hooliganism were public enemy number one across Europe if not the globe. The top clubs, aware the required massive stadia refurbishment would cost huge amounts of money sniffed the possibility of greater television cash even more so. For that to happen, English football needed more credibility, for the good to outweigh the ugliness. Fortunately Italia 90 went a long way towards providing this.

England's run to semi final penalty heartbreak captured the public imagination. Paul Gascoigne provided the skill in midfield that The Three Lions had lacked for years and have done ever since. Millions were glued to their television sets, not just football fans. I remember watching a game round a previously non football loving friend's house and trying to explain the offside rule with the aid of salt shakers and sauce bottles.

"But surely the ketchup is playing the pepper pot onside." He said. I gave up after a while.

Despite missing out on the final, England received a remarkably large and rapturous homecoming. The Italian 1990 World Cup is part credited with making football more accessible to those who had forsaken the game and also introducing new converts. Sometimes these are known as the middle classes or prawn sandwich brigade. They echoed a growing feeling that the football entertainment experience was changing.

The pie and Bovril days were coming to a close. What wasn't known was, a few decades later this would lead to sky high admission prices, poor atmosphere, and tourists more intent on taking a photo of the action than watching it. That's the thing with a brave new dawn, you never know what the day will bring.

For instance, you would never have bet that one of England's almost heroes would end up being Coventry City manager with months of the 1990-91 domestic season. But that's what happened when after a mediocre start, John Sillett was axed and replaced by England's central defensive kingpin, Terry Butcher.

The board of directors talked of a need for a change in direction. So Sillett went after a four year period of constant league stability. A duration of which we hadn't experienced before in the First Division and wouldn't again. Perhaps Sillett was too loyal to certain players in a age where loyalty became more of a rarity.

Butcher, reaching the end of his playing career and injury prone, played just seven league games. He struck lucky in that one of the last acts of the Sillett transfer in activities was the signing of Kevin Gallagher. Fast and sharp he netted seventeen precious times for his new club. Gynn also hit a purple patch scoring 11 times. The problem that emerged with Butcher's reign was you couldn't see any coherent style of play or set tactics emerging.

The best game of the season came when Nottingham Forest were floored 5-4 in the League Cup on a remarkable Highfield Road night. The stadium again seemed at its best under lights. Not that Nigel Clough saw it that way as he scored a hat trick yet still finished up on the losing side. In January, Speedie departed for Liverpool. Kenny Samson now too like Butcher approaching his closing playing days joined the Sky Blues.

City finished sixteenth. The jury was out on Butcher. In summer, Regis departed for Aston Villa. It said a lot about the esteem in which he was held, there was very little of the usual acrimony over a loved player leaving for a local rival. The wind of change that seemed like a storm in the distance now gathered momentum. While clubs didn't know for sure until February of 1992, they were to taking part in the last season of football as people knew it.

City got off to a pretty decent start including a win at Highbury and at home to Villa. But things turned pretty grim. Gallagher lacked support up front. City were still relying on the scouting system to throw up basement buy bargains. Two such players were new central defensive partnership, Peter Atherton and Andy Pearce. Plucked from lower climes, they did a pretty decent job although some credit for that has to go to Don Howe who Butcher brought in as first team coach.

Howe's tactical knowhow some him accumulate an impressive CV at club and national level but he had a reputation for being dour, reserved and unadventurous. Despite that, on January 6th 1992 he took over the Highfield Road hot seat after a dismal run of results left the club six points from the drop zone. The board had taken a gamble and failed. So now worried about their place in the brave new world they acted. Butcher was dismissed.

It said a lot about the state of football back then that for the home match with Chelsea, City gave free tickets to the unemployed. Such a fixture would probably set you back fifty notes plus nowadays. I was out of work then and gratefully gained free admission. Some of my fellow UB40 clutching Sky Blue fans sung to the supporters from West London, "You've got a penthouse and we're on the dole."

Things were slow to pick up under Howe with a string of draws keeping us out of the quagmire. That included four successive godless stalemates as many a City fan uttered, "Typical Don Howe." The formation of a new Premier League had been unveiled on February 20th including the top 19 teams in the ongoing season's top division. For ultimate survivors Coventry never was their renowned Houdini act more important.

After a fraught run-in, a win over West Ham in the last home game set up another last day cliffhanger. Despite losing at Villa naturally to a Regis goal, other results went our way. We were in the promised land. One that would no longer be shown live on terrestrial television, as in May, satellite broadcasters Sky won the TV rights. The casting vote is said to have been made by soon to be Tottenham chairman, Alan Sugar. Sugar also owned the company producing the dishes for Sky. So all above board in the brand new era then.

Some years later it emerged that BBC and ITV had for some considerable time been operating a cartel that kept highlights package payments etc lower than they might otherwise have been. The Football League itself for decades went into full flap mode over live matches having an impact on attendances. So you could say, everybody got what they deserved.

Sky were promising to revolutionise the way football was broadcast live. Like any leap into the unknown some were twitchy. Perhaps the directors of Coventry City were among the nervous as in the summer they sensationally announced the return of Bobby Gould to the club. This time it would be as joint manager with Howe. The job share never materialised as Howe left before the start of the season leaving Gould to take sole command.

Bobby clearly felt he had unfinished business at Highfield Road. By July, Sky were ramping the hype up to the max in a concentrated attempt to sell shed loads of new viewing subscriptions. Our household decided to pass on it, not keen on what became the done thing, paying a fair old wad for what had been previously watched for free. Sky were snapping up other sports. They blew BBC out of the water in the bidding for televised England cricket rights. Change had arrived and seemed unstoppable and unwatchable unless you set up a Sky direct debit.

Coventry City were still in there with the elite. In truth, nobody knew how things would pan out. Sky introduced the slogan, "Its a brand new ball game." Like football had been born again. All they had to do now was convert enough believers.

Live Forever Premier League 1993-2001

The New Testament had arrived. When Brian Deane scored the first ever Premier League goal, its announcement came with tones suggesting this was akin to the first goal ever scored. Like history had begun again. Three games in, for years had been the acceptable mark to produce the first proper league table of the season. I began to like the idea of rewriting history as Coventry City topped the Premier League table, having won all three of their opening matches. The Bobby Gould kick-start effect had worked again and we were off to a flyer.

Talking of which, Sky used planes to fly over grounds pre kick-off. Parachuters would land on the pitch with the match ball. Live match analysis had never been done with so much depth. Their coverage was brash and bold. If it looked a little self indulgent, Sky cared not. The concept being sold was, this slick presentation represented the way of the future. And you'd be a fool to miss out.

Six wins and two losses from the first eight fixtures for Coventry suggested anybody thinking the new era would belong solely to the big boys were mistaken. Aston Villa and Norwich got off to excellent starts too, with Manchester United also showing strongly. I went to see City entertain Blackburn with my Dad, the first time we'd attended a game together in years. Despite an Alan Shearer inspired Rovers being too strong for us, Dad had the bug once more and we went together as father and son to numerous matches again after that.

An eight match winless run saw City slip down the table. Gould tried to address this by bringing in striker Micky Quinn on loan at first then permanently from Newcastle. The barrel chested marksmen made a wonderful start, scoring in his first four matches. After six games, Quinn had netted ten times. On fire didn't cover it. A classic goal poacher in the purest sense, Quinn had neither lightening speed or staggering skill. He just harboured an uncanny ability to sniff out where scoring opportunities would fall and stick them away with admirable ruthlessness.

Another player given his chance by Gould and causing a stir was young Peter Ndlovu from Zimbabwe. Spotted by Sillett but signed by Butcher he had bewildering pace and skill. The downside being Peter was so unpredictable he didn't know himself what he would do next, leaving his teammates with little chance of reading his intentions. Small wonder he didn't get promoted to the first team until after the departure of Howe.

I first saw Ndlovu in the reserves, matches attended by a few hundred people. His breathtaking individual runs, beating players while running at full pelt, drew genuine gasps of admiration from those present. A good foil for Quinn, the pair were instrumental in some outstanding results.

Villa were hammered 3-0 at Highfield Road but that paled in comparison to the visit of Liverpool who were on the end of an unbelievable 5-1 thrashing. Moneybags Blackburn were not immune either as City went to Ewood Park and romped home 5-2. The Sky Blues had also introduced the speedy John Williams into a forward role. Known as the flying postman due to his previous occupation and past record of being a champion sprinter, Williams again offered something defenders had rarely encountered. A pace packed rawness without fear.

The trio of new offensive weaponry persuaded City to accept a bid from Blackburn for Kevin Gallagher. Sadly after

March 3rd the all too familiar late season form slump occurred. The side won just one more match all season. That came at home to Southampton. I watched with amusement as Quinn, a mad keen horse racing fan continually looked up at the scoreboard for the result of The Grand National, which took place that day or rather didn't. The whole field jumped the gun in the mother of all false starts and the race had to be rerun on the Monday. Quinn looked more and more perplexed as he glanced up for the result that never came.

The last fixture of the season versus Leeds, was the last played in front of City's famous terrace, The Spoin Kop. A new stand would be built behind the goal. It genuinely saddened me that the end that held so many memories would be no more. All stadiums were going to be all seater in the wake of the standing tragedies that had blighted football. I understood this but was still filled with melancholy at the loss of the terraces. For what to be represented a hub of working class culture with a real history beyond sudden invention.

City finished 15th. Once again a season that promised so much had petered out into mediocrity. Manchester United won the inaugural Premier League, their first top flight title win in over two decades. The general consensus was the new dawn looked like being a massive success. Homes and pubs alike were snapping up Sky dishes. Like it or not, the revolution was well under way and would be televised, as long as you subscribed of course.

Statisticians were scratching their heads and researching the record books big time at the start of the 1993-94 season. Perplexed at the last occasion an opposition player went to Highbury and bagged a hat trick. That's exactly what Mick Quinn did as City stuffed The Gunners on opening day to get the campaign off to a sensational start. The first eight games were unbeaten although this record did contain five draws. One point out of the next twelve on offer culminated in a 5-1 hammering at QPR. But still nobody expected what happened next.

The shower water in the dressing room had barely stopped running when an extremely emotional Gould announced his resignation. You always got the feeling that his close affinity with his home City club brought more pressure on him and that he expected his passion to be shared by players and board alike. Gould clearly felt that with some of the directors particularly this wasn't always the case.

His assistant Phil Neal was handed a chance to prove he could cut it as a managerial number one as ably as he'd worn the number two shirt at Liverpool for many years. Things got off to a modest start but Christmas and new year wins at Wimbledon and Tottenham lifted spirits. An injury to Quinn limited him to 27 games and nine goals in the league, two less than top scorer, Ndlovu. American international forward Roy Wegerie arrived at the club. A skilful player although not prolific goals wise.

Neal favoured hard workers like Sean Flynn, Steve Morgan and David Rennie. Phil Babb at centre back looked a stylish player of much potential. Some fans were not enamoured with Neal's pragmatic style. I sat next to one guy who regularly, game after game would berate Rennie. After we'd conceded one soft goal the boo boy screamed, "That's Rennie's doing again. Can anyone tell me why he's on the pitch?"

"He's not. He's on the bench." I correctly and gleefully informed him.

"It would have been his fault if he were playing." He said, prejudice intact.

City closed the season unbeaten in eight to finish a credible 11th. This run included a fine Highfield Road Easter win over Blackburn that ended their title hopes and handed the crown to Manchester United for the second successive season. Sky audiences continued to grow. Many grounds were being revamped. Often one end resembled a building site or was covered by a boarded mural by the more inventive such as at Highbury.

In 1994-5, I continued to attend some of the home games with my Dad when his shift work permitted. We enjoyed the many pubs that were in the area of Highfield Road. Good old fashioned boozers and social clubs who made a financial killing on match days. We met and made a lot of friends and had a good drink. We'd often say the day out at the football was only often spoilt by the football.

That season, the first full one under Phil Neal proved a fraught affair. Just three games in, the manager and Quinn had a major bust up. In that scenario there is only one winner and Quinn never played for the club again. He did leave some good memories and to his credit was a genuine cult figure which our fans needed. His replacement, brought in by Neal, proved one of the most important signings in the history of the club.

Dion Dublin endured a miserable time at Manchester United. Injury wrecked his big opportunity at a massive club. A bloke they signed called Eric Cantona also proved an obstacle to him making the first team. Dublin proved an instant hit at City. He top scored with 16 goals. Ndlovu contributed 13 valuable strikes but the next best scorer had three goals which tells you where a major problem lay. The midfield under Neal became based on grafters, work rate making up for creative limitations.

Results were mixed and City were pretty much rooted in the bottom half looking over their shoulders at the strugglers. City chairman Bryan Richardson was an openly ambitious figure who had brought into the Sky dream era. He wanted to continue to be a part of it, raise the club's profile and his own. Neal's days were numbered from the time, Ron Atkinson recently sacked by Villa, started attending games at Highfield Road, almost stalking Neal's position.

Finally, Big Ron replaced Neal and Gordon Strachan came in as player assistant boss on the understanding he would eventually take over the reigns. The move duly got City onto the back pages. City had enough in hand to stay up, their status secured with a good win at Spurs in the penultimate game. Atkinson wasted no time wheeling and dealing, bringing in his own experienced men like Kevin Richardson and David Burrows.

Richardson and Atkinson were a good match, both loving the limelight and intent on staying there. With rich Labour MP Geoffrey Robinson on the board, the investment so denied so many City bosses looked likely to bankroll Big Ron's squad rebuilding. Players that were better not just battlers were promised to the fans. Big words from big characters. Now all that was needed was big deeds.

Atkinson spent much of the summer reshaping the playing staff. Richard Shaw, Paul Telfer and John Salako cemented regular first team places together with Paul Williams who had arrived from Derby towards the end of the previous campaign. However, there were less successful recruits such as Eoin Jess, Nil Lamptey and the Brazilian, Isaias. It's arguable too much change was made too soon. But City struggled from the off.

Me and Dad spent an early season game at home to Arsenal sitting next to two blokes who said they were the Bedworth Gunners, the town's Arsenal contingent,
"Just the pair of you?" I asked.
"Our other member is on holiday." One replied deadpan.
After a win against Man City in the first home match City went on one of the most fruitless runs in their top echelon history. This lasted until December 5th. We were rooted at the bottom until three points finally arrived in unfathomable fashion when visiting champions Blackburn were on the wrong end of a 5-0 thrashing in Antarctic conditions. Dublin proved again the main source of goals.
To try and help him out up front, Noel Whelan came in from Leeds. An highly promising young striker, he instantly made a mark. His individual goal in a draw with Southampton went down as one of the best solo efforts seen at Highfield Road in some time. It spawned a mini revival. But for all the increased expenditure the campaign had a very familiar feel about it. A raft of draws kept us in with a shout of safety, more dour Don than Big flamboyant Ron.
Somehow this seemed to galvanise the atmosphere at home where there were two nail-biting single goal wins over Liverpool and QPR. The home crowd backing being superb, seemingly singing us to a safe haven. But other relegation battlers picked up points too. This season which started off with much fanfare from the board was to end up like so many others, with a last day do or die decider.
Leeds were the opponents at Highfield Road. The veteran fans of many last gasp cliffhangers went through the usual array of emotions. At the end of an excruciating goalless ninety minutes, Coventry had stayed up on goal difference. Home fans invaded the pitch, away fans invaded the pitch.

And one of the biggest punch ups in recent times ensued as the rival contingents fought each other.

This kind of summed the season up. A tale of frustration, tension and unrealised potential. You looked at the individual players and they seemed to be better than what we'd had. But something, somewhere was missing. Gordon Strachan due mainly to injury rarely played. But in his few appearances, in the twilight of his career, clearly no longer physically at his best, his footballing intelligence showed up the others.

We bit the bullet at home and brought a Sky dish and subscription. Some big foreign stars were now making the Premier League their own. Kevin Keegan's superbly entertaining team somehow blew the league title from a very strong position. It again went to Old Trafford. The new Sky TV dawn was now in full effect. But for City, despite the bluster, more investment, the story remained the same.

It had become obvious the Sky Blues were crying out for more midfield creativity. Someone also seemed to decide a marquee signing was required, a statement of ambitious intent. The result being the transfer in of Gary McAllister. Captain of Scotland and Leeds with one of the most cultured left pegs in the game. Paying over £3 million for a player was excessive by Coventry standards yet alone shelling out that grand sum for a player over the age of thirty.

Leeds fans were unhappy, branding McAllister a money grabber as better wages were somewhat surprisingly on offer at City. Richardson and Atkinson were delighted with the signing. The plan being the new experienced playmaker would fit in nicely with a team that had already had a season to gel. 1996-97 would see real progress. The plan had one fault. We looked more horrendous than ever, in fact much more so.

The first alarm bells rang as early as a prestige pre season friendly at home to Benfica. A good result against a renowned quality team would set up confidence nicely for the season ahead, reasoned Big Ron. The Portuguese giants ran out 7-2 winners. Within moments of the big kick-off itself, visitors Nottingham Forest looked faster, fitter and far more confident.

"This is going to be a long hard season."

"We are going down for sure."

Those words are always uttered when a team concedes first on opening day. But this time, the prophecy looked frighteningly real. A Kevin Campbell hat trick sentenced us to another heavy defeat. This signalled one of the worst starts to a season in the club's history. A win against Leeds in early September saw the only three point return until a week before Christmas.

By that time, Atkinson had been moved upstairs with Strachan taking complete charge of the first team. Big Ron didn't last long in that always contrived managing director role. He missed the dugout too much. As he did literally, in taking over Nottingham Forest and sitting in the opposition dugout. Pinpointing what went wrong under Atkinson isn't easy when you look at the players he brought in. When that happens, fingers point inevitably at the manager.

Some quotes attributed to Atkinson offer clues.

"I think Ndlovu is best in the loose cannon role."

"I told Borrows he was the man to go man to man on McManaman."

Perhaps these Ronisms confused the players.

Strachan brought in a striker called Darren Huckerby from Newcastle. He couldn't get a game in the Geordies reserve team because bizarrely they didn't have one. Effectively replacing Ndlovu who'd gone to Birmingham, Huckerby was a breath of fresh air. Fast and confident in his dribbling ability. He could be very exasperating too. Often caught offside he received a memorable back handed compliment from Strachan who said, "On his day, Darren is a world beater. On another, he's a carpet beater."

Embracing the positive side of his game, Huckerby proved inspirational as City celebrated Yuletide with four wins in a row. Results after that were patchy though a great win at Anfield raised hope. Then Chelsea were defeated at Highfield Road while weirdly wearing City's away kit because they'd forgot their own. But things were so tight at the bottom, it became clear. You're never going to believe this, but Coventry's fate rested on a last day relegation decider.

For City it became dreamland. For Sunderland, a nightmare revisited. Our final game at Spurs had a delayed kick off. Can you see where this is going? City triumphed 2-1 at Spurs in the mother of all heart attack inducing matches. All over Wearside, effigies of Jimmy Hill were rumoured to have been burnt. The pubs that night were resounding to that hollow but celebratory last gasp reprieve feeling. Someone uttered the phrase that had become our mantra, "If the Titanic were Sky Blue, it would never have sunk."

The fact of the matter remained we were back where we were for much for much of the eighties. Richardson vowed it would never happen again, Strachan echoed his words, lessons would be learnt.

During the summer he brought in Swedish international, Roland Nilsson. Another member of the thirty something club but nevertheless the right back soon showed his class. A cultured defender of style and intelligence. Although much younger, Irish lad, Gary Breen looked to have the same promise as he established himself in the Sky Blues side during 1997-98.

The season got off to a flyer as Chelsea succumbed 3-2 in a Highfield Road thriller. This proved a personal triumph for Dublin who netted all three goals. Again there were too many draws early on but gradually City started to look better even though McAllister picked up an injury that ruled him out for a long period.

Me and Dad were now regulars in the North Stand. The football we played was of a higher quality and Dublin's partnership with Huckerby began to terrorise defences. Though pretty opposite and no means on a telepathic wavelength like Ferguson and Wallace, something clicked.

Things turned a bit dodgy around November when City lost six games out of seven. It didn't bode well for the Christmas time home clash with Manchester United. I had a job then working as a seasonal temp at Debenhams. There was a decent chance of a full time contract if my attendance was good but I'd already lost a few days. So I gave my ticket to my brother thinking the game would be nothing special. How wrong can you be?

Coming back from a goal behind to beat the side United had back then was special enough. But the winner by Huckerby went down as one of if not the most memorable of Highfield Road Sky Blues goals. Picking the ball up just inside their half, he weaved his way through the United defence and midfield for that matter, at pace. Then the ball crisply left his foot and hit the neck to clinch a stunning win. I consoled myself missing out by videoing the game on Match of the Day and replaying it constantly.

More importantly, the improbable triumph served as a catalyst. Seven straight wins on the bounce in January and February ended the possibility of a struggle like the last two seasons. Also, the ultimate bonus ball occurred. One of the biggest monkey's on the back of City fans had been their inability to win at Aston Villa.

Not once in their long history had City supporters travelled the short distance up the road and came away victorious. Romanian striker, Viorel Moldovan wrote himself into club folklore. Brought in to add competition up front he netted the only goal of the game. After twenty seven visits to Villa Park the supporters in Sky Blue finally had local Derby bragging rights.

And I also missed this famous victory. This time it was because of a dead parrot! I'm not going all Monty Python but the pet parrot of a girl I was going out with at the time died on the morning of the game. She was really upset so I didn't go to Villa Park. Consolation came as we progressed to the last eight of the FA Cup and a winnable looking tie at home to second division, Sheffield United. Richardson came up with the ruse that everyone had to buy a programme to get in which annoyed a few people.

City turned in their most disappointing performance for a good while in a 1-1 draw. The replay was shown on a big screen in the East Stand concourse at Highfield Road so I went to that. Dublin who had been playing at centre back due to injuries stayed there even though the crock list had eased. It proved a mistake as another tight mistake ridden game ended in another stalemate. Groans went up everywhere as we lost on penalties. A great opportunity for that team to make their name had been missed.

It affected league results. Six out of the last nine matches were drawn denying us a top ten finish. Although eleventh place was pretty decent in context of the previous couple of campaigns. Dublin finished with 23 goals in total and got picked in the preliminary World Cup squad for France. But along with Gazza he didn't make the final cut. Joint Golden Boot winner Dion, could also fill in at the back ably should there be suspensions but it still wasn't enough for Glenn Hoddle.

Although the Sky revolution had really taken off there was still trouble. But that now mainly took place outside the grounds due to better segregation and greater police numbers. This gave Sky the somewhat sanitised image their cameras were seeking inside stadiums. Against Forest the previous season on opening day, I'd saw a mass battle by The Hastings pub after the game.

Then a good few hours after our home game with West Ham, we rubbed up some old school East End Skinheads the wrong way and got chased all over the show as they suddenly produced knives. You find you can run rather fast in those circumstances.

We were on a night out, walking to a bar near the train station. You have to go through a subway and there was a lad lying on the ground being given a kicking by a couple of these West Ham skins. Dave Lanchbury was with us and he knew one of the mate's of the injured party and he is asked to help. So we ran at the East Enders who legged it through the subway towards the station. We helped the lad up and called an ambulance for him.

But then these enraged manic skinheads ran back through the subway at us waving blades. They chased us all over the show. Thankfully they were slowed down by their clumpy Marten boots and we made it to safety. I've rarely enjoyed a pint as much as I did after that little episode.

On the last day of the 97-98 season, Dave Lanch went to our final game to Everton. They were in dire danger of going down but escaped when it ended one all. Dave said the mood at Goodison Park completely changed when we scored the equaliser. Another City goal would have sent them them down and produced an anger so great, it was the only time he'd ever been glad we didn't win.

Inside grounds, plush new stands were springing up everywhere, stadiums were generally more family friendly. Bryan Richardson felt if City were to progress, then they had to move to a bigger arena with greater capacity. Plans were underway for construction of our new home, a grandiose sporting amphitheater on the outskirts of the City. Initial drafts even had a retractable roof but this notion was later, er, retracted. Funded by the council, it would see the sale and demolition of Highfield Road to make way for a new housing estate.

To be honest, I was horrified. HR had been part of my childhood, adolescence and so on. But we were being sold a dream. The Premier League continued to flourish. Anything seemed possible. In those circumstances, you buy into things that in some ways are unpalatable. For when some get the scent of money, other senses dull. Right now we were part of a runaway success story. No one thought to ask the basic question, what if the wheels come off?

Good Riddance (Time of Your Life) 1998-2001

Chelsea must have thought lightening really does strike in the same place twice on the first day of the 1998-99 season. Just like on the previous campaign's curtain raiser they came to Highfield Road and lost, this time, 2-1. Dublin and Huckerby were at their best that day. Me and Dad walked home full of expectation of good things. Football though has a funny habit of raising your hopes then kicking you in the teeth. Just a few weeks later, our stroll back was in speechless disconsolation following a 5-1 tanking from Newcastle.

Even more gloomy disbelief arrived when Dublin departed for Aston Villa. Having announced his wanting to leave, a cluster of clubs came in for him though none of the big guns as he would obviously have preferred. So a move to our local rivals didn't go down well with the fans. For my part, I didn't harbour him any animosity. He had a brilliant goal to game ratio for City at a time of great change in football. And for me, Dion Dublin was one of the primary reasons we were still there.

Rather than replace the striking talisman despite banking over £4 million, Noel Whelan became Huckerby's foil. It never worked as well as a partnership and winger Steve Froggatt brought in to provide service for Dublin was somewhat wasted. Dutch midfielder George Boateng looked a class act though and City embarked on a season of regular ups and downs. The highlight undoubtably being ending our Villa Park League hoodoo by a crushing 4-1 margin.

Villa started with eleven English players that day. It's some twenty years later as I write this, and that statistic still stands. Which says a lot rightly or wrongly about the way the domestic game has gone. Liverpool who often had a bad time at Coventry once again left empty handed. But City couldn't string a decent run together. They missed the physical presence of Dublin. Whelan certainly put himself about even though he had more to his game than that and top scored with thirteen, one ahead of Huckerby.

I went to Old Trafford and it struck me how corporate things were becoming. There were people outside the ground giving out leaflets for personal injury and PPI claims. A long way from when I first started attending football and political extremists would hand out flyers.

This game also saw me almost create a first by causing a fight by breaking wind! I let one rip in the away stand and two City sitting behind me fans accused each other of being the guilty party. They nearly came to blows as neither would rightly admit it. A gentleman would have owned up so I didn't.

The Sky Blues finished 15th, failing to push on from the progress of the previous season. But as we'd known for many years, if you sell and don't replace your best players that is what happens. We were still a decent side, capable of giving the best a game but as seemed perennial, lacked consistency.

Plans for the new stadium gathered momentum. I became a bit of a serial writer to the local paper, questioning some of the ideas involved. For instance, the catering and car-parking profits from the new ground would not go to the club. We would rent from the council, be mere tenants, never to own our own home. To me the proposals had more holes than a cheese grater. I also satirised Richardson and

Strachan too, to a lesser extent. I felt the chairman talked big but was taking us into a high risk venture with no get out clause or turning back.

Strachan for me, was a frustrating coach, tactically naive, with no real plan B. He had his favourites who would be picked no matter what. I did and still do enjoy his dry wit but questioned then his managerial abilities at the highest levels and think history has proved me right. The pace the game was now moving at meant you couldn't stand still on and off the field. On the field, we were close but stagnating. Off it, we'd boarded a ride with no breaks.

I once read an article in a football magazine entitled, Coventry City, What's The Point? It scathingly questioned the existence of a club, the writer felt whose sole aim was to stay in the top division, survive and very little else. Harsh I thought but I accepted the basis behind the viewpoint.

After one match of the 1998-99 season, Huckerby departed for Leeds. Again, when the bid came in, he wanted to go. I think Strachan had always been as confused as he was enthralled by Darren. Such a player is a test for a coach. Because you want to erase his frustrating aspects but risk losing what makes such a player different and dangerous. This time, Richardson knew the fans demanded a replacement.

That player was Robbie Keane who became the most expensive teenager in football when he joined City for £6 million from Wolves. From the early minutes of his debut at home to Derby you could see we'd signed a special talent. Keane had skill, balance and an exquisite first touch. He scored both of the game's goals. City had also signed two Moroccan players, Hadji and Chippo. Both looked decent although much more so when things were going well.

After years of being first choice goalie, Oggy lost his place to Swedish keeper, Magnus Hedman. McAllister was now back to full fitness pulling the strings in midfield. Often, in a City shirt, you'd see him hands on hips looking forlorn at other players not being able to respond to his vision. Keane changed all that. For one so young, he timed his runs from deep to perfection.

Newcastle and Watford were on the end of Highfield Road wallopings. Some of the stuff we played at home was scintillating. The highlight being a thrilling 3-2 Boxing Day win over Arsenal. After a two each home draw with Chelsea shown live on Sky, presenter Richard Keys labelled City, "The entertainers." We will ignore the fact, he may have been slightly biased being a Coventry born lifelong fan of the club.

Away form though held us back. We simply couldn't win on our travels. The FA Cup seemed the best chance of success when we reached the 5th round and drew second division Charlton at home. Even more so when were two up at half time. We lost 3-2. Gutted, I went home to write another angry letter to the local rag. I berated Strachan's tactics which I felt were awful that day. The new stadium plans were in progress and the surely obvious flaws remained. That had me constantly hounding the Coventry Telegraph letters page too.

Our last chance to win away came and went with a goalless draw at Watford. This direct contrast to fine and exciting home form saw us restricted to a 14th place finish. For the last home game, a 4-1 win over Sheffield Wednesday, Oggy was given a chance to say farewell to the fans he'd served so well. 507 appearances, a magnificent testimony to his consistently. They also included one goal, ironically at Sheffield Wednesday.

Despite our away woes, me and Dad were optimistic. The majority of home matches had been a joy to attend. The side contained flair and with hopefully a few quality additions on the horizon the future looked bright. Little did we know that football's version of the unsinkable Titanic had set fare collision course with its version of the iceberg.

"This is going to be a long hard season."

"We are going down for sure."

Once again the soothsayers of gloom were out in full force when we timidly capitulated at home to Middlesbrough on day one of 2000-01. In truth, before the campaign had even started, fans were left shellshocked by the sudden sale of Robbie Keane. After less than twelve months at the club he was the subject of a surprise £12 million pound offer from Italian giants, Inter Milan. Richardson and the board decided to cash in.

This gave further fire to a rumour that abounded. This being the "race horse theory." That a consortium including certain directors were funding transfers in and reaping rewards when they were sold on for profit. This notion became further inflamed when Whelan departed for our first day opponents, Middlesbrough, just days later. The rumour remained just that and was never substantiated.

McAllister had already left for Liverpool in July. Out of contract at City, the lure of spending his final years at Anfield was too good to turn down. He had some good moments in a Sky Blue shirt but you felt often lacked people on the pitch around him on the same wavelength. Better players play better with better players. That surely is obvious.

Fans were unhappy despite the big money arrival of Craig Bellamy from Norwich. After a fine season at Carrow Road, a bad injury had ruled him out for months. Now Richardson and Strachan gambled he'd be fit and confident enough to replace two key strikers. Gritty yet skilful Liverpool squad player, David Thompson also joined and a promising debut display against Boro was wrecked when frustration boiled over and he received a red card.

Yet in typical City fashion, the first two away games were won. Two more than we'd managed in the previous season. Perhaps the panic was premature. Or perhaps not. We managed three more wins before Christmas although Boxing Day brought a fine victory at Everton. But on December 16th, I went to fellow strugglers Derby. We got beat 1-0 but there seemed more to it than that. We looked short in every department. I'd never been so worried and that's saying something.

The attack consisted of Bellamy playing out left wide, isolated and unable to influence the game for long periods. Inexplicably, Hadji was employed as the main central striker. He looked way out of his depth.Surely an out and out forward would be brought in. But the weeks went by and it didn't happen.

The midfield also appeared a long way short, Thompson maybe the exception but without much help. Defensively we looked vulnerable and nervy. Hedman in goal showed fine reflexes but didn't command his box like Oggy. He got injured and rookie goalie Chris Kirkland came in. Full of promise but cruelly exposed.

After the victory at Everton, it took until March 31st for another three point outing. By then our fate looked sealed. Far too late, muscular but clever striker, John Hartson, came in. The impact he had was immediate. Another win followed at Leicester. With Hartson beside him, Bellamy looked a lot more comfortable.

Even the only win we had in that spell, at Swindon in the FA Cup caused me grief. Me and Dave Lanchbury went to a pub owned by a Coventry fan who lived there but it was some way from the ground. We ended up on Swindon's notorious magic roundabout with kick off fast approaching. So we pulled off and left the car on a housing estate. Following the match, we couldn't remember whereabouts we had parked, walking round for what seemed like an age before the motor finally appeared in front of us.

With six games left there was still a mountain to climb despite the mini revival. A home win against Sunderland was sandwiched by two defeats. Gary McAllister predictably scored the goal for Liverpool that virtually sealed our fate. He looked as upset as the home fans when his free kick effort went in. The penultimate match was at Aston Villa. The horribleness of the script there for all to see. Going down there of all places.

A 3-2 defeat finally put City out of their misery. It had been an abject campaign. Three quality players shipped out before the season had barely began and nowhere near adequately replaced. Strachan sold short by Richardson, stayed remarkably loyal to him shouldering the blame. In truth, he imploded himself in very difficult circumstances. Surely a change of manager while we still had a chance of survival was worth a shot. It had worked before but the board were too stubborn and blinkered to change things.

The 34 year long proud at the top drew to a close with a final day scoreless stalemate against also relegated Bradford. A meek swan-song after all those many final game end of season dramas. I maintain that relegation was wholly avoidable. Aided and abetted by weakness in the dugout and boardroom alike.

After all those years in the top flight we merely wimped out. I don't think the board grasped the magnitude of the situation despite the impending construction of a lavish new stadium.

One we wouldn't own, wouldn't get any profits from. For me, mismanagement was everywhere.

Strachan was to last just five games during the next season. Richardson didn't fare much better being ousted in a vote of no confidence in late January 2002 in a boardroom coup. His human shield gone, his natural optimism belied by the harsh reality of the ultimate results business, previous allies turned against him, People who were as culpable as the chairman in voting with Richardson on the lemming like clauses in the stadium contract now booted him out.

Sisu rightly get a lot of stick for their reign at City but the seeds of prolonged demise were sown long before then. In a boardroom where blind ambition, and one man's ego ran rampant until it was too late. History tends to bury questions that are not asked at the time.

Like in terms of money in from transfers, where? The inadequacy of fiscal provision for the club in the new stadium deal, why? We will never know whether incompetence played a major part or something else. But supporters of a club with a prolonged top flight history were surely sold down the river.

One guy at Villa Park famously waved a banner proclaiming, "We'll be back" It seemed fair enough. We'd been up there long enough to believe a return wouldn't be that difficult. But what we didn't know was we had not just dug ourselves into a big hole. Things were much more serious than that. The chasm in the coming years became the very edge of the abyss.

Smile Like You Mean It 2001-2007

Home defeat in Grimsby in early September saw Gordon Strachan leave Highfield Road. The first five games had yielded just four points. During an August bank holiday Monday home clash with Nottingham Forest the atmosphere verged on poisonous. Unable to beat a side reduced to nine men the furious crowd turned on Strachan big style. It couldn't go on and didn't. But not before, in the close season, Strachan had spent a large percentage of the relegation parachute money on Lee Hughes from West Brom.

Richardson turned to Roland Nilsson who came in to manage the team and play as well. Results slowly but surely picked up. The highlight being a thrilling 4-3 home win over Manchester City. I had just dislocated my shoulder and sat in the North Stand with my arm in a sling. The doctor told me to completely rest my ligaments while the shoulder healed. Easier said than done when your witnessing a last gasp winner. I instinctively put my hands in the air when David Thompson got the deciding goal and reeled in agony.

The home clash with Portsmouth unexpectedly made headlines way beyond the back pages. I was standing outside the Brew and Baker pub when a Pompey mob rushed down the street out to confront anyone in Sky Blue. Looking for all the world like an organised outfit, they goaded any set of home fans in sight. City supporters somewhat put out, began to react.

That culminated inside the ground where swathes of opposing fans fought ongoing pitched battles in the West End seats. This was near where home disabled supporters were situated. The fighting went on for some time. Few police were in attendance with a low key occasion expected. Later, rumour was, a notorious Pompey firm had arrived en mass seeking revenge for an incident involving one of their number being injured previously by a Cov lad. Portsmouth's premier firm, the 6.57 crew denied this.

On the pitch things were rather more mundane. Lee Hughes struggled for the form and goals that had given him legendary status at West Brom. The side couldn't seem able to find any coherent pattern of play. This wasn't helped by a string of loan players arriving. Mike McGinnity had took over as chairman and announced the club's financial position was worse than previously thought. Cheap fixes were being sought.

This didn't go down well with supporters. Neither did his short-lived idea of changing the club's much loved badge. City flirted with the play off places and six wins out of eight in February and early March gave us a good chance. At the Norwich home match I had free tickets after winning a poetry competition. This was when I at last met my boyhood Tommy Hutchison who presented my prize.

One point out of the last twenty one available consigned City to a disappointing 11th place finish. With a few games to go, promotion hopes gone, Nilsson got the boot. His replacement, another familiar face, Gary McAllister. He would manage and play, fresh from a short but multi trophy winning spell at Anfield. We seemed to be grasping at straws. This became something Coventry fans would get well used to.

Hughes soon returned to Albion at the beginning of the following season. City supporters had found their own new cult hero in Bosnian centre half, Mo Konjic. A huge strapping central defender of the old school variety, his no nonsense approach became richly appreciated at a time when nonsense was rife. With Mo in partnership with Richard Shaw we looked half decent at the back through pretty toothless up front. Jay Bothroyd took the main striker mantle but never really impressed at City like he did at future clubs.

The play off's looked a possibility until a disastrous second half of the season. One solitary game was won after Boxing Day as City went from promotion contenders to finish 20th. If the season had lasted a few more weeks we would have gone down. The spell included a series of insipid performances bordering on embarrassing. I witnessed one, an FA Cup exit at Rochdale which was as disgraceful as I've seen from the football club.

To try and halt the decline, McAllister brought in a raft of journeymen pro's. This seemingly endless list of mainly loans revolved around a core of a handful of players who featured in most matches. A pretty desperate policy thrust upon him by cutbacks. In just two years, City had plunged down from the Premier League to scraping to stay up in the second tier. Reality had kicked in and it felt pretty grim indeed.

The board pledged loyalty to McAllister. Midfield hard man Micheal Doyle arrived. His tough tackling competitive qualities represented something that had sadly been lacking. Julian Joachim originally signed by Strachan but plagued with injury, was given the task of scoring the goals. But again, mainly loan players were the order of the day again for 2003-04. The problem being for every decent borrowed player like Stephen Warnock there was a plethora of mediocrity.

Things could hardly get worse but the improvement belonged to the middle table also ran variety. In January 2014, the announcement came that McAllister was leaving to nurse his sick wife. To his credit, he had soldiered on with such harrowing personal problems. But family comes first and in a sense it was a relief for all because things clearly hadn't worked out as positively as hoped for.

The board turned to assistant manager Eric Black. He put more emphasis on neat short passing football with attacking intent. There were some entertaining matches and we dispatched a few teams with high scoring aplomb. There was too much ground to catch up on but we'd improved to 11th place. The players had responded to Black. The fans had responded to Black. The directors and chairman responded to Black by announcing he was being replaced by Peter Reid.

With bizarre timing, Reid came in for the last game of the season. McGinnity said we needed a proven manager and the chance to employ Reid was too good to pass up on. Again, the fan base expressed dissatisfaction. The way it had been handled ensured Reid would have less of an honeymoon period than is usual. A lot of supporters thought they were being taken for granted, their views not listened too. Although this was something becoming increasingly prevalent in football.

The division was rebranded as The Championship for the following season. Obviously for commercial gain but I've never been convinced by this. If you're in the second division of a league no name change can elevate the standard or make it any more exciting. It rather patronises the punter instead.

Reid brought in the experienced Tim Sherwood who spent so much time injured it was said they were going to rename the Ryton treatment room after him. This did have a blessing as it allowed Stephen Hughes to form a useful midfield partnership with Doyle for much of 2004-05 and beyond. The goalscoring burden would mainly fall on new recruit Stern John and promising young Cov born attacker, Gary McSheffrey.

From the start, results were indifferent. Encouraging wins were followed by disappointing defeats. This was the last year of City playing at Highfield Road before moving to the new 36,000 capacity stadium. The directors had obviously brought Reid in to mount a promotion challenge with the big move in mind. But it just wasn't happening. In fact, we were again looking nervously over our shoulders at the drop zone.

The best I saw City play under Reid's tenure, was with ten men for much of the match at home to Crewe. Stephen Hughes had to go in goal after Ian Bennett got sent off. We were superb but still lost 1-0. The players were applauded off suggesting, despite the harsh treatment of Black, they wanted Reid to succeed.

By early January after just two wins in eight games, Reid was gone. Rightly, he could say he didn't have enough time. The board would argue time was the one thing they were short of such being the desperate need to return to the Premiership with the stadium move being on the horizon. Some fans thought Reid should never have been appointed in the first place. Whatever the rights and wrongs, on the Sky Blue managerial roundabout, it was once again time to shout, next!

Step up Micky Adam's. City again turned to an old boy for what was rapidly turning into one of football's hottest managerial seats. Having gained good varied coaching experience at Fulham and Leicester, Adam's looked a good fit for City. Brought to the club as a player by Bobby Gould, he was a fully committed figure during that spell at the club.

I decided to try and go in each end of the ground for our last season at Highfield Road. Against Crewe in the FA Cup, me and my mate Andy Scobie went in the West End seats. A bitterly cold day felt apt as the ghosts of many past matches in the old terraced West End flashed in front of me. Kind of rites of passage where you grew up quickly during turbulent times for the young football fan.

Adams endured a difficult start which landed us on the periphery of the relegation places. The supporters rallied round, the atmosphere being electric during invaluable home wins over Brighton and Nottingham Forest. Relegation in our last Highfield Road campaign would have been an unthinkable end. The very thought of it seemed to spur on the players too.

By the time the last ever home game at the much loved ground arrived we still weren't completely assured of safety. I brought tickets for me and Dad in the North Stand. Appropriate we went together there for one last time in tribute to all those years after he first took me up. In the early days he used to say I had Sky Blue eyes as I would never hear of any criticism of the club. That changed but I hoped I didn't end up fighting back tears just as I had on my first ever Highfield Road visit.

I do actually have blue eyes and they were welling up towards the end. But with tears of joy as a magnificent 6-2 victory banished relegation fears and ensured the day became that of pure uninhibited celebration. The years rolled by in front of us. From the optimism's of August's to the cold realities of past January's and all those narrow early May escapes. With a heavy heart it was time to say goodbye to Highfield Road.

Young Andrew Whing had the honour of scoring the last ever goal at the stadium. Kind of apt that a product of the youth policy, the one constant that served so well, entered the record books with the final strike. My Dad was never an emotional man but I could see the feelings within him that day, no doubt recalling how he used to go to Highfield Road with his own father.

Fond goodbyes said, the time had come to move on. It was announced our first three games would be away from home as the Ricoh as it would be sponsorship named, wouldn't be ready in time. Straight away you see another significant development in football. Stadium naming rights. Grounds named after companies who produce goods such as printers in the hope of printing money.

On August 20 the Ricoh Arena hosted its first Coventry City home game, a 3-0 romp over QPR. I went with my Dad to the admittedly impressive new stadium for the first time against Reading. Sadly he never took to the new ground at all. Struggling with his mobility and the greater travelling distance, it was difficult for him and he never went to the Ricoh again after City's first season there. It saddened me but he'd always say, "It's a brilliant stadium but it just doesn't feel like home."

And that was the problem for myself and some other football fans over the years. You can put up statues outside the ground, but you can't just tap into tradition and history. It's that which makes older grounds special with almost a church like place of worship feel. New arenas have sprung up all over the Country. Works of fine modern architecture, spacious, family friendly but ultimately cold and lacking in passion.

Whether the move had any adverse effect on the players is debatable but by December we had won just three games. Pressure was already mounting on Adams Then McGinnity resigned the chair on health grounds being replaced by Geoffrey Robinson, who made no secret new investors even owners would be considered at the club. On field,

McSheffrey provided our main threat despite again being played out wide. Stern John and Dele Adebola weighed in with most of our other goals but the midfield area was light on support in this area and that of creating chances. A common problem over the years.

But things picked quite dramatically as a fine spell of Ricoh results became the basis of a revival. Sadly the early dismal run meant the play offs were beyond us but an eightieth place finish brought hope. The catalyst for the turnaround of the club's season could largely be attributed to the short term signing of veteran Dennis Wise. Eleven appearances brought six goals. Like Strachan, his legs may have gone but his footballing brain remained very much intact. Sadly he left after that cameo spell at the club.

For 2006-07 Adams brought in a number of new recruits. Goalkeeper Andy Marshall, winger Chris Birchall, forwards, Leon Mckenzie and Kevin Kyle. But he did lose McSheffrey just a couple of games in when he departed for Birmingham. A consistent scorer from out on the flanks, this was a blow to Adams who didn't hide his disappointment at losing the player.

Yet again, we didn't kick on. The supporters at home games particularly grew frustrated. Any new stadium boost had waned. The walk to the ground filled with anticipation soon turned to moans once inside as things went wrong again. City were rooted in mid-table. Robinson announced City's financial situation had became dire. This was nothing new. We were often told of a couple of minutes to midnight situation at the club.

Hedge fund Sisu emerged as potential new owners. A mysterious set-up fronted by ex Man City defender, Ray Ranson who seemed a genuine footballing man. With City being apparently minutes from entering administration a deal was struck. One of the provisos was every share would be owned by Sisu. For years, a number of supporters had owned a couple of shares. It made them feel part of the club. Now they were told, give them up or there will be no club.

It fell to City director and long time loyal Sky Blue servant Joe Elliott to collect the stray shares, taking to visiting people's houses to do so. Being a shareholder, even a single figure number meant a person could attend the club's annual general meeting. There the directors could be called to account for their actions. This would no longer be the case.

A new regime at the helm makes a manager vulnerable. Fresh owners often want their own man in charge of team affairs. So the last thing Adams needed was the dire run that coincided with the takeover. A dismal winless streak in the league extended to a pretty spineless home FA cup exit to Bristol City. This also saw the lowest Ricoh attendance so far. A day later, Adams was sacked.

He fronted up the cameras well as he left the ground for the last time. Very emotional, insisting he did his best and remained proud of it. The England team manager's task is known as the impossible job. But being in charge of Coventry can't be far behind. Following a interim period with Adrian Heath holding the fort, it was announced Iain Dowie would be the new City boss.

At Crystal Palace, he took over when they were 19th in the First Division table. A magnificent run took them to 6th and a place in the play offs. This led to a win at Wembley that secured a stunning promotion to the Premier League. Although unable to keep them there and with a short unsuccessful spell at Charlton on his CV, Ranson decided

Dowie would be charged with taking City back to the promised land.

A good run of form promptly followed before a equally bad trot of results confined the Sky Blues to a 17th place finish. Big on player statistics, diet, modern training methods, Dowie promised things would be different once the squad got used to his criteria. Ranson meanwhile held a number of meetings with fan groups. These were intended to allay fears about the intentions of a seemingly otherwise faceless hedge fund.

Ranson however smiled and connected affably with supporters. He said a detailed redevelopment strategy was underway at the club. Some fans thought he fielded questions in the manner of a politician. Style above substance that being but the general consensus was he had knowledge of the game and how it should be run behind the scenes. The thing being, the precarious state Coventry were in fans had very little choice, trust issues or not.

Fix You 2008-12

God knows, Coventry fans hadn't had much to cheer about for longer than they cared to remember. So even merely being drawn at Manchester United in the League Cup was greeted with real enthusiasm. The regular campaign had started in promising fashion with ten points from the first four games. Over ten thousand fans travelled to Old Trafford. For some younger followers, this was their first experience of a top class stadium cup tie against a club laden with trophy winning history.

Despite fielding a weakened team, United were red hot favourites. But the next day the back page headlines belonged to a diminutive City striker from Malta called Micheal Mifsud. His two goal blast without reply sealed a famous victory that sent the away hordes into raptures. At last, long suffering Sky Blue supporters had a night to remember.

Mifsud proved a bonus for City in 2007-08. Small and tricky, somewhat selfish but determined he troubled defences. Like many players of that ilk over the years for City he was stuck on the wing. A fate that also befell Andy Morrell for much of his time at City despite being a fairly prolific down the middle striker for much of his career elsewhere.

The Old Trafford upset didn't have much of a positive knock on effect in the league. Dowie had spent a fair wad on Gary Borrowdale, Jay Tabb, Leon Best and Elliot Ward. Kevin Kyle departed after a miserable time at City that left supporters saying they'd have been better off with Jeremy Kyle. Form dropped off after the bright start. City were marooned in no man's land. Every win that looked like providing a springboard was followed by a losing knock-back.

One thing football boardrooms have become ever increasingly short of in modern times is patience. On February 11th, Dowie was "released" from his contract. Differences between manager and board about the way forward for the club were vaguely cited by both parties. As is the modern way, a cloak of confidentially descends when coaches depart. Like the severance package partly funded by fans is none of their business.

Before Dowie had barely left his office, new boss, Chris Coleman was sitting in his seat. Following a successful stint at Fulham, Ranson said it represented quite a catch for the club. Coleman acted quickly in the transfer market bringing in Scott Dann and Danny Fox from Walsall. But poor results continued unabated. Despite a last day walloping at Charlton, City stayed up due to other results, finishing a bitterly disappointing 21st.

Coleman reacted by continuing to reshape his squad. Highly rated keeper Kieran Westwood came in together with Icelandic midfielder Aron Gunnarsson. Coleman also recruited fellow Welshmen, Freddie Eastwood and David Bell. Bell sadly went on to rival Tim Sherwood in the most time spent in the treatment room sweepstakes. The team now one he could call mostly his own, Coleman said he was quietly confident of a top half and pushing on season.

Ranson continued to meet with fans, talking of his vision for the club. When I started going to football, you barely knew of who sat in the boardroom. Jimmy Hill is largely credited with Coventry's 1960's success but it was funded by then chairman, Derrick Robins. Despite being something of an extrovert character himself, he gave Hill both the cash and the spotlight.

Nowadays it's more difficult. Supporters want to know who are the owners are but don't want over interference. Sums invested however can be colossal so naturally some owners are very hands on. Coleman fended off any off field questions insisting he was purely a football man. As such, he would be judged on results. And once again, they could only be described as indifferent. The highlight of the season was a run to the FA quarter finals before defeat to Chelsea in front of a packed Ricoh.

But in bread and butter matches, City fired a lot of blanks. Eastwood couldn't find the form that had given him cult hero status at Southend. Morrison looked and proved around a dozen goals a season striker rather than the twenty plus required. In fairness, he lacked service. That the player making most headlines for City was goalie, Westwood, said a lot. Defenders Fox and Dann also received critical acclaim but Coventry limped to a 17th place end position.

Gates at the Ricoh continued to fall particularly for midweek evening games. Stuck on the north M6 edge of the City, the Ricoh suffers from traffic gridlocks that makes travelling on public transport undesirable. I went to the Cardiff home night match that season. I live about five miles from the ground and have to get two buses. I left at six o'clock and missed the 7.45 kick off. I'd got to Derby much quicker by getting a lift by car.

The fans had been promised good transport links. What they did get was exorbitant car parking fees. But with the way things were, that was nothing to do with the club because of the long term arrangement made with the council and private companies. Ranson spoke of frustration at not owning the arena. Rent money being dead money at a sum agreed when City were a top flight club.

Coleman suffered a blow when the club quickly cashed in on Dann and Fox. That Ranson too professed disappointment made you wonder just exactly who was pulling the strings. In fairness, money was made available to Coleman who continued to stamp his mark on the staff. Martin Cranie, Micheal McIndoe, Sammy Clingan and Stephen Wright arrived to become mainstays of 2009-10.

And it did lead to improvement from our woes of the previous two league seasons. The problem being, we now looked bang average as opposed to inferior. Football is all about opinion of course, and it's my view, Coleman rates as one of the poorest manger's I've seen at City and heaven knows it's a hotly contested accolade. I know he lost Dann and Fox amongst others but he had a decent playing budget yet the squad both personnel wise and tactically always looked short.

After struggling in the autumn of 2009, his side did find a bit of form. Three consecutive December successes brought cheer then after a new year stutter, February and March saw five wins out of six. Suddenly, we were a couple of places off the playoffs going into an important Ricoh clash with Cardiff. Optimism turned to anger as City sheepishly slumped to a 2-1 loss.

Not one single game out of the last nine saw victory as City went into free-fall. They'd gone from contenders to a final position of 19th. In the last home game with Watford, Coleman angered large sections of the crowd by denying defender Marcus Hall a farewell appearance in a match that meant nothing to us. A local lad who had two spells at the club, Hall had given good service mainly deployed at left neck. It seemed churlish not to allow him the chance to say goodbye.

On the following Monday, Coleman cleared his own desk and said his own farewells as he was sacked. Within a fortnight, Aidy Boothroyd had been appointed as his successor. With a similar background to Dowie, Boothroyd had surprisingly led Watford through the playoffs to the Premier League.

Now he had the job of satisfying both disillusioned supporters and impatient owners at Coventry. He talked well although had a reputation of being something of a long ball coach. But by now City fans didn't give a hoot about attractive football by then, they just wanted winning football.

So again a new manager spent the summer reshaping the squad to his own specifications. Lee Carsley and Gary McSheffrey returned for second spells at the club. In a bid to add firepower, Lukas Jutkiewicz and much travelled Clive Platt were recruited together with defender Richard Keogh. He and Richard Wood tightened up the centre of defence at the start of 2010-11.

Although rarely on the scoresheet, Platt benefitted from Bothroyd's direct tactics troubling defences and creating opportunities for Jutkiewicz. City were looking a meaner outfit than under Coleman and entered autumn in the playoff places. 28,000 attended the Ricoh to see Leeds win 3-2. This was the first of three defeats on the trot followed by three wins keeping City right in the mix at the right end of the table.

Whenever City got within sight of the top six, the television pundits would gleefully remind viewers we hadn't achieved a final finish there since 1969-70. It had grown unto one of the most unwanted long running statistics in football. For a few brief weeks it felt like nosebleed territory to see the league tables with a continued Sky Blue top six presence.

That progress then got somewhat overshadowed when the decision was taken to offer a contract to Marlon King. The striker had just been released from prison having been convicted of sexual assault. Because of this, his contract had been terminated by Wigan. Bothroyd had worked with King before at Watford and invited him to train at Ryton.

When the announcement came King was to be offered playing terms, opinions divided. Some thought it disgraceful tainting the club's standing while others argued he deserved a chance. I thought I'd sit on the fence by sitting on my hands if he scored. And he did score, pretty regularly. Some were won over by this, others stuck to their original stand of opposition.

Whether the divide had any impact on the players is debatable. On December 10th, King scored the only goal of the game from the penalty spot at home to Middlesbrough. After that yet another manager presided over yet another barren set of results. Just one win until mid March saw yet another manager relieved of his duties. With more than two years left of his contract and the club slipping precociously near the danger zone, Bothroyd got sacked. And the fallout didn't end there.

Shortly after, the club announced they were under a transfer embargo for failing to meet transfer payments. Two weeks later, Ranson quit the club. His replacement was Sisu's Ken Dulieu. Although Ranson was rumoured to be greatly frustrated by practices undertaken by the owners, the truth never emerged due to what appeared to be a confidentially agreement between the two parties. This would become an ongoing feature of the Sisu reign.

Amongst the chaos, coach Andy Thorn became caretaker boss. As is so often the case, results almost immediately took an upward surge. 11 points from a possible 15 saw the

Sky Blues climb out of the mire. The players seemed to be thriving on a more succinct on the deck passing style. It brought the best out of recent recruit, Carl Baker a stylish but grafting midfielder with a goal scoring knack.

By the end of April, Thorn had been appointed permanent boss. I went to the last home game, a goalless draw with Reading. Despite all the shenanigans, a sense of optimism prevailed. Even the dreaded Mexican Wave went round a stadium lit up by a Sunny May day. Perhaps some of this was fuelled by a feeling things simply couldn't get any worse. Which just goes to show how wrong you can be.

Brian Clough had legendary strong views on the input of chairmen and directors. That being they put in the money and no other input is required. So Cloughie would have been stunned like most Coventry fans when director Leonard Brody mooted the idea of, text a sub. Yep, supporters being invited to send texts suggesting who the manager would take off and bring on.

There's a scene in Blackadder where he says to the pompous out of touch general, "Have you ever considered visiting planet earth Sir?" That pretty much summed it up.

Due to the embargo Thorn could only sign out of contract players. He snapped up goalkeeper Joe Murphy who had been released by Scunthorpe. Carsley had become under 18's team coach. After a long running saga, King signed for Birmingham leaving the side looking meagre up front. To be blunt, numbers and quality looked slight all over the park as 2011-12 kicked off with a Ricoh defeat to local rivals Leicester. To appease this, there were good home wins over fellow Midlanders, Derby and Forest.

The problem being as Coventry supporters sat down for Christmas dinner, they were the only two victories gained so far in what had become a calamitous campaign of monumental proportions. A two points from possible thirty run saw City marooned at the bottom of the division. Dulieu had quit as had Brody. It was never confirmed if Sisu were accepting text suggestions for his replacement.

In an equally daft idea, Dulieu had joined Thorn in the dugout for one game. I would really liked to have seen how Clough would have dealt with that scenario. Two home festive wins lifted the gloom temporarily. We soon returned to losing ways. Although the general consensus amongst fans seemed to be Thorn should have gone by now, he drew sympathy for having his hands tied by transfer restrictions.

Instead the wrath of some supporters was aimed directly at Sisu. A protest took place by Jimmy Hill's statue outside the Ricoh when Southampton visited for an FA Cup tie. Proposed takeover bids by a consortium led by local businessman, Geoff Hoffman were resisted. But resentment and suspicion over the current owners grew. Such a poisonous atmosphere could have only made things more difficult for the beleaguered Thorn.

He wasn't helped when Jutkiewicz left for Middlesbrough in the January transfer window. It had been hoped Cody McDonald would be the answer to the goalscoring conundrum, when he'd signed for City at the end of August. Prolific for Gillingham he managed only three in the league that season for the Sky Blues. Although, again he was feeding on scraps in a side bereft of any penetrative edge.

In March a mini revival saw seven unbeaten games although only two wins. A relegation six pointer showdown at Bristol City ended in defeat. I followed the match on my laptop, slamming it down on the table when the final whistle went. The screen went a weird colour then liquid poured out of the top of it. It was kaput for good. This seemed like a fair comment on our season.

On April 21st, the inevitable became reality. Following defeat at Doncaster, Coventry City were relegated to the third tier of English football. Despite looking out of his depth, Thorn's services were retained for the hoped for promotion push. Hands tied by circumstances beyond his control, Thorn's brand of neat tidy passing football was exposed as toothless.

Again as with the first relegation I'd experienced under Strachan, it felt wholly preventable. In the modern game, no manager no matter the backdrop can expect to survive results like those delivered under Thorn. A new face at the helm often leads to a turnaround in form and results.

A lot of people with to who the club means everything had a right to feel shortchanged. Yet hardcore City fans are a very loyal breed. Even following the most horrendous of seasons they were talking of new grounds to visit, of bouncing back despite everything.

I joined Twitter during that season and saw passion, anger, resignation, admirable loyalty. But above all people who care. And there is no substitute for that by text or otherwise. Now we were right back where Jimmy Hill had dragged us from. The hope was we had found a level from which to crawl back from. The free-fall surely couldn't continue. Little did City fans know this was nothing compared to the coming storm that would threaten the very existence of a much beloved football club.

Crack The Shutters 2013-17

Not surprisingly the summer of saw a mass exodus of the playing staff. A dozen players left although Thorn brought in a number of his own recruits in due to the transfer embargo being lifted. This enabled him to reshape the squad for a crack at an instant return to League One. The amount of players he was allowed to sign suggested the board still had a lot of faith in him.

Yet after three matches, all drawn, Thorn was dismissed. A sluggish start to 2012-13 admittedly. But given that he'd been permitted to reshape the squad after the previous disastrous season, it felt odd. Thorn came across as a decent bloke but one faced with situations and circumstances that far more experienced managers would have struggled with.

Richard Shaw and Lee Carsley were placed in temporary charge but results got even worse. By mid September, City were at the bottom of the old Third Division. Grim times indeed. The board turned to Mark Robins who had gained plaudits for his stints at Rotherham and Barnsley. He came across well in interviews. Robins was given a three year contract at a club where twelve months at the helm practically qualified for a long service award.

Robins lost his first game at home to Carlisle. However slowly but surely began to turn things around. He had a bonus in the form of striker David McGoldrick brought in by Shaw on the last day of the August transfer window. He featured prolifically on the scoresheet as City shot up the league. In just a few months the Sky Blues went from rock bottom to the edge of the playoff places.

Travelled but highly rated forward, Leon Clarke arrived to add more firepower. In addition, we made decent progress in the Football League Trophy. By the new year City had reached the Northern area final. The away following had been superb and over thirty thousand turned up at the Ricoh for the first leg of the semi against Crewe. This highlighted the potential of a fanbase starved of success. Sadly, they witnessed a crushing 3-0 defeat that scuppered hopes of a first Wembley appearance since 1987.

The future looked a lot brighter though. But in the world of Coventry City things are never that simple. The supporters were rocked as the news broke, Robins was leaving to become manager of Championship club, Huddersfield Town. Maybe he knew what was on the horizon as just over a fortnight later, City were again placed under transfer embargo for failing to file accounts. Some fans branded Robins a Judas, others saw why he wanted a more stable environment.

The thing was, as a supporter it wasn't like supporting a normal football club. You were constantly embedded in politics. One crisis seemed to follow another. This escalated after Steven Pressley joined the club as manager from Scottish club Falkirk where he'd done well. Within weeks, City were placed into administration. Then all club staff based at the Ricoh were moved out as a long ongoing row between Sisu and stadium owners ACL spiralled out of control.

The club's owners had long thought the rent too high and wanted an option to own or part own the ground. This fell on deaf ears. The two parties were miles apart on many issues. City chairman Tim Fisher had even threatened to move the club out of paying at the Ricoh, even the City as things turned ever more ugly.

Any chance Pressley had of continuing the playoff push were shattered as the Football League deducted the club ten points for entering administration. With that body blow he decided to concentrate on building a side to challenge for promotion the following season. City finished 15th. They appealed the deduction decision and withdrew that appeal just days later.

When you talked to your fellow CCFC supporter friends, there was far more than football on the agenda. This was typified when administrator Paul Appleton put the club up for sale in the summer of 2013. Four bids were received. Appleton announced the most acceptable was from a company called Otium Entertainment Group. Their directors included Ken Dulieu and Leonard Brody also directors of Sisu. We had effectively been sold to ourselves.

Then on July 3rd came the announcement that would send the club into turmoil. With all negotiations having broke down between Sisu and ACL for our continued presence at the Ricoh, the club said all "home" games for the next three seasons would be played at Sixfields, home of Northampton Town. Fisher acknowledged gates would fall but stressed there was no other alternative. He didn't forecast a greatly significant club threatening fan drop off.

Outrage ensued. A well attended protest march took place. Large sections of fans proclaimed they would boycott City fixtures at Sixfields. The phrase, Not A Penny More, was born, from a section of supporters insisting they wouldn't put any money into Coventry City while Sisu remained.

Other fans said it wouldn't stop them going despite being deeply unhappy about the situation. Fan was set against fellow fan over the moral rights and wrongs of watching their own team. Surely one of the most stressful and despicable scenarios foisted on a set of supporters anywhere.

Then on the eve of the season Pressley received a massive blow even before a ball had been kicked in earnest. City were again deducted ten points. This time for exiting administration without a CVA. On the same day, Otium were awarded the golden share for the coming season. Cue social media meltdown as enraged fans vented their outrage.

The first game of 2013-14, a 3-2 defeat at Crawley saw Coventry fans invade the pitch to highlight their plight. The first fixture at Sixfields was attended by 2,204. The previous season's average Ricoh gate was 10,950. Fishers prediction was bang out. Some fans took to watching this and following games at Northampton standing on a large hill which overlooks the ground. Watching from afar while holding protest banners.

Some fans boycotting even tried to persuade those going in from doing so. A situation had been created akin to football's version of the miners strike. It put people into a place nobody should be in, questioning the very ethics of going to a game. Friend disagreeing with friend, arguments raging while the football authorities reacted with deafening silence.

The game against Bristol City, in absolutely typical Coventry City contradictory style, was a scintillating affair finishing 5-4 in our favour. I never saw it having opted not to watch City at Sixfields. The idea of a football club being based outside its home locality was not one I felt I could tolerate. I did however ponder what decision I would have made if the situation had arose when I first left school and hardly missed a home or away game.

The tragedy was that at the outset of the campaign the club uncovered a diamond from the youth academy in striker Callum Wilson that some never saw in Sky Blue. Sharp with electric pace, he grabbed with chance offered to him by

Pressley. In partnership with Leon Clarke, they were a real handful for defences.

Another Sixfields thriller saw a four all draw with Preston. The goals of Wilson and Clarke shot City up the table despite the points handicap. Scottish midfielder John Fleck also began to flourish with his fine passing ability. Eight goals though were then conceded in heavy defeats at the Northampton ground, by Tranmere and Rotherham. Before the Sky Blues bounced back with a good 3-1 win at MK Dons.

The away following in Milton Keynes clocked in at 6,781. Nearly three times the number attending matches at Sixfields. This summed up the madness that had engulfed the club. Well over five thousand also made the glamour trip to Arsenal as the club made the FA Cup 4th round but were predictably walloped. Early form subsided with just four wins in the last twenty games. The start of this slump coincided with the sale of Clarke to Wolves in January.

Pressley employed the in vogue high pressing style without the ball. This was coupled with a patient approach when in possession. But as the season wore on, the impact of this tiring full on mental and physical approach waned. With ten points taken off the score board from the off, City limped to 17th place. Although most clubs handed a double figure starting deduction would probably settle for that.

More worrying for the Sky Blues was, the missing thousands from Sixfields were finding other things to do with their leisure time. Take two friends of mine, Chris McMilan and Gary Drinkwater. They bleed the club colours but decided Northampton wasn't for them. Gary became a leading sponsor at Coventry speedway while Chris indulged his love of retro pop at music festivals. Some took to putting their money and time into local lower level teams still based in the City such as Coventry Sphinx. A few even set up an alternative club, Coventry United.

Haemorrhaging fans and money, there seemed no way the club could survive the contracted three seasons playing at Sixfields. The owners had took the council to court, ACL to court, lost cases and appealed them. This must have cost a lot of money.

Fans on social media began to target the head of Sisu, Joy Seppala. A reclusive and enigmatic figure, it wasn't even known for sure if she had ever attended a City game. Fisher was the public face of Sisu and as such took some fearful stick. This intensified when Wilson was sold to Bournemouth. For the second close season in a row, a summer demonstration march attracted an impressive turnout.

Things looked grimmer than ever as the opening game of 2014-15 was lost at Bradford. A decent seven game unbeaten run followed. In the midst of it, came the most welcome news in ages. Following intense behind the scenes talks, it had been agreed Coventry would return to play home matches at the Ricoh Arena. Quite what hammered open the locked shutters of communication between the warring factions wasn't clear. It hardly mattered. City were coming home.

Over twenty seven thousand fans attended the homecoming despite the game being on a Friday night live on Sky. They were suitably rewarded with a single goal win netted by Frank Nouble. The jubilant atmosphere must have been particularly rewarding for Pressley. He had turned down an approach from Huddersfield for their vacant managerial post. Given what he'd been through at Coventry, you wouldn't have blamed him for going when his stock was still high, unaffected by the shambles around him.

Within days of going back to the Ricoh, there came an announcement that Rugby Union club, Wasps had purchased the stadium in a surprise long term deal. So this wrecked any hopes Sisu had of owning the arena themselves.

Questions were asked of the Council about how a facility built for the city of Coventry could be sold to a London based set up. Wasps attempted to allay concerns by saying they were moving to the City lock, stock and barrel and the stadium would continue to serve Coventry people. Sisu responded by, you got it, launching a court case.

The feel good factor of the Ricoh return didn't impact on the pitch for long though as results slowly declined and City slid down the table. With little punch up front, Pressley's ball keeping emphasis bordered on tippy tappy tedium. At one bitterly cold home 1-1 draw with Fleetwood, I could see his system disintegrating with players not capable or confident enough in it to deliver his plans.

After exactly 100 games in charge, on February 23rd with the club dropping towards a perilous position, Pressley was sacked. It looked justified in that he'd took City as far as he could. That this was back to square one league position wise, doesn't reflect how he managed a beleaguered club with dignity and integrity during its darkest hours. You could only wish him well.

City handed the reigns to Tony Mowbray. He had a decent CV and a reputation for producing attractive footballing sides. But survival was his opening brief. During that season a bewildering amount of loan players arrived. A good number of these were to try and break the goal drought that ultimately saw Nouble top score with a meagre seven. Loanee Dominic Samuel chipped in with an invaluable 6 in

12. But Mowbray struggled to get any sort of run going from a squad short on quality.

After a home loss to Port Vale, I watched a few young away fans dressed in Burberry trying to organise a ruck with Coventry counterparts. Speaking calmly into his mobile phone, a lad said things like, "Fair enough, we'll have you then. See you soon." I felt like a old man watching a modern day firm politely setting up confrontation.

I wanted to tell him, "In my day, you just mingled in with the crowd and ambushed them." But I'd have felt akin to Uncle Albert in Only Fools and Horses and his "During the war" ramblings.

Mowbray joined the long list of City bosses who have sweated on last day survival. A goal by promising academy graduate, James Maddison sealed escape at Crawley. A new generation of fans went into raptures based on relief that we weren't going into the lowest level of league football. I have to say, City's committed away day following in the lower divisions deserve immense credit for their loyalty and loud support.

Singers Corner at the Ricoh has also vastly improved the atmosphere. Mainly young and very vocal fans gather by the scoreboard and voice their commitment to City. Chants and songs abound no matter the state of the game. This is direct contrast to some of the older fans at football these days who seem to thrive on a mood of negatively.

Singers F.C. was the first ever name of the club that became Coventry City F.C. So there is a good sense of history there. The initial name Singers derives from a make of push bike that was manufactured in the City. It was the hub of bicycle manufacturing before going on to be the heartland of motor car building. Works team, Singers, formed by Willie Stanley eventually became the Sky Blues

During summer 2015, Mowbray adopted a policy of bringing in on loan, hungry youngsters from higher level clubs. Adam Armstrong, Ryan Kent and Jacob Murphy all came in. Veteran Sam Ricketts arrived and was made captain by Mowbray. Eight players were shipped out. Personally, I'm not a big fan of extensive use of the loan system. I believe it is still possible to construct a team mainly of your own signed players and this leads to continuity and greater team understanding.

But I have to say, Mowbray's trio of talented borrowed kids really hit the ground running, especially Armstrong. He netted five times in the first three games, which yielded a full nine points. City stayed nicely camped near the top as autumn came. The team played some of the most attractive entertaining football seen at the Ricoh and away for some considerable time.

In late October, the club brought in a surprise well known name in Joe Cole. One of the best midfielders of his generation, he quickly heaping praise on the set up. Fellow promotion chasers Gillingham were destroyed at the Ricoh. City entered the new year in a great position and began 2016 by thumping Crewe 5-0 on their manor. Every time you spoke to another City fan in the pub, talk was upbeat. For once we looked the real deal.

I saw a couple of those familiar old prophets of doom on social media relate how Mowbray's side at Middlesbrough had been in a similar position and bottled it big time. Surely that wouldn't happen to us and some people are looking for bad omens during good times. A poor FA Cup home exit to non league Worcester somewhat dampened the mood but the getting out of League One remained the main and highly feasible priority.

Five matches without a win was ended by a colossal 6-0 home stroll over Bury. But suddenly it happened again. The second half season mega crash that had plagued City so often. Ten games without a win saw us tumble out of the top six. Fans previously delighted with things under Mowbray voiced their dissatisfaction. The youngsters in the side visibly drained of morale.

Despite four wins out of the last five fixtures, there was too much ground to make up. After being nailed on for at least the playoffs if not automatic promotion City finished 8th. If you looked at it logically this meant massive improvement from the last day escape of the previous season. But logic plays no great part for fans who finally thought they'd banished the curse of no top six finish for decades on end.

Mowbray remained calm though obviously bitterly disappointed. We'd made progress and would go again. But the summer recruitment was uninspired. Armstrong had scored over twenty times during the last season but returned to his parent club Newcastle, as did Murphy to Norwich. From the very first game you looked at the team and bench and it looked wafer thin.

Maddison had been sold to Norwich in February for a big fee and add on's. Now, we were selling players before they'd even given decent first team service, like a feeder club. Maddison was then immediately loaned back to the club for the rest of the season. I thought he was a bit underused for his talent.

Not one victory was delivered by the Sky Blues in the first ten matches. On September 29th a late goal by AFC Wimbledon earned them a point at the Ricoh. Just over eight thousand people attended. Immediately after the match, a club statement revealed Mowbray would no longer be manager of Coventry City.

His assistant Mark Venus was made caretaker boss with view to the position on a permanent basis. This appointment seemed somewhat unusual as he'd also been appointed onto the board of directors. A board where fresh unknown faces arrived and disappeared with frightening regularity.

His first game brought a win at home at Port Vale. Then during the following outing at Charlton, both sets of fans held a joint protest against their respective owners. Ten points from a possible twelve gave hope but then six reverses on the spin followed. During the Sky televised home loss to Sheffield United, anti Sisu protests were prevalent throughout culminating in a group of fans invading the pitch. Chairman Fisher stormed out of the directors box as the cameras honed in.

On December 21st, City appointed Russell Slade as manager. He lasted just over four months during which one solitary league victory was gained and relegation all but assured bar a miracle. Slade's tenure had been an utter disaster.

Yet unbelievably, the new manager would have the chance to lead Coventry out at Wembley. The Football League Trophy renamed The Checkatrade Trophy that season had saw City turn their league form on the head to reach a final at the National Stadium for the first time since 1987.

The competition had been revamped in a much maligned new format. Clubs from the top two divisions were allowed to enter the competition in the guise of their under 21 sides. Or should that be disguise, as managers opted to give some players in their mid 30's a runout undermining any good intentions the misguided change had. Some fans disenchanted by the now contrived nature of the competition called for a boycott. This led to some pitiful attendances.

Typical of Coventry City then, with their worst side in decades, in their worst season ever, to reach the final. Supporters seized the chance to support their team and showcase the club's vast potential. Despite everything that had occurred, the club shifted in excess of over 40,000 tickets for the Wembley game with Oxford United. A collective determination ensued to show the Sky Blues at their best rather than recent television images of desperate protestation.

The turnout could have been even higher. Some I spoke to did chose not to go because of their disillusionment with Sisu. Others had a feeling they would be hypocritical after mercilessly barracking and parodying the strange new makeup of the tournament. One clearly drummed up in those strange ivory towers where football's decision makers live in their fantasy land.

I didn't go but not for reasons of objection. I'd been ill for a good few months preceding the final, losing weight, strength and balance. As City reached Wembley, I was diagnosed with Parkinson's Disease and placed on medication together with a period of convalescence. But that was just the tip of the iceberg. My Dad had also been very poorly for some time with doctors unable to find out what was wrong with him. Then around the time of the Checkatrade Final, my Dad was diagnosed with terminal motor neurone disease.

Suddenly I realised that at times like this, football fades into insignificance. Yet in a way that makes it more important. The game was the glue that brought me and Dad together, gave us a common bond and social outlet. It brings family generations together in a way only seen at invited kin gatherings where you often attend just out of politeness and etiquette. Age and generations gaps are rendered void by football.

Coventry's starting eleven for the final would be picked by Mark Robins. Just when you think nothing can surprise you in football, it surprises you. Eyebrows were raised when hours after Slade's dismissal, Robins was unveiled as his successor. The fans were mainly welcoming. With all the turmoil that further exploded at the club, after his initial departure you were more surprised he wanted to come back.

But Robins was adamant he could work with the board. It looked way too late to turn the league season from hell around but there was still the possibility of winning a trophy. Giving long suffering fans something back. Showing the world there was yet life in a club practically on life support. A social media clamour for Oggy to lead the team out at Wembley was taken on board. The loyal stopper then long serving goalkeeping coach received the deserved accolade of walking out the players. The one constant in a ever shifting tide of madness.

A stunning total of 43,000 Sky Blue clad fans went into raptures as Gaël Bigirimana slotted home the opening goal of the match. Apt reward for the popular young midfielder in his second spell at the club. A rare highlight of Thorn's ill fated only full season in charge, he returned to City after a big move to Newcastle saw him mainly sit on the bench. Youngster George Thomas increased the lead. Ironically, this would lead to a big move to Leicester where he wouldn't even get near the bench.

Oxford pulled one back but this Wembley day was always going to belong to Coventry City. An oasis in a barren desert of years of just when you thought things couldn't get any worse, they got a lot worse. When the final whistle sounded I felt particularly pleased for the youngsters such as those who gather in Singers Corner. At least the older fans had the triumph of 87 or the Jimmy Hill days. But the latest set had nothing of note and deserved their day at English football's most revered venue.

I watched the match in the house with my Dad. Sadly he was rapidly losing the ability to speak by then. So there was barely a murmur from him when City scored. I felt sad that at the end of his life, City were about to plunge into the fourth tier where we'd resided during his early days as a fan of the Bantams as we were then nicknamed.

Thirteen points adrift with half a dozen games left gave Robins no chance of redeeming the league season. In the end we finished eleven points from safety at least avoiding the wooden spoon. That brought no consolation from a truly shocking nine months. Mowbray appeared to implode and quite why Venus and Slade ever got the gig is beyond comprehension.

So Coventry City had fallen from the heights of being 34 years long members of the top flight to what is the fourth division by whatever name it may be called. A story of neglect on a grand scale. Robins had to get us back and fast you felt. The man credited with once saving the job of Alex Ferguson now had to rescue a club in danger of slipping off the football map altogether.

We'll Live and Die in These Towns 2017-18

Rumour has it, Robins ordered the World's biggest skip to get rid of the deadwood accumulated by his predecessors. Nine players left during summer with more following as 2017-18 progressed. A new midfield engine room arrived consisting of Liam Kelly and a familiar face in Micheal Doyle who came back to wear the skipper's armband. Defenders, Jack Grimmer and Rod McDonald were recruited together with a new strike force of Marc McNulty, Max Biamou and on loan from Wolves, Duckens Nazon.

But it was highly rated but under pressure to deliver, Jodi Jones who lit up the opening match with a hat trick to no reply against Notts Country at the Ricoh. Just the start that was needed but then three of the next four league games were lost. In addition, City crashed out of the League Cup. While new French creative force Tony Andreu picked up a sickening injury in just his third game that ruled him out for the season before August had closed.

But Robins adopted a mood of calm and asked supporters to do the same. Five out of the next six were won with three goals were conceded. It soon became clear the new template would be a ultra mean resolute defensive unit further protected by Kelly and Doyle. Their skills at keeping possession were to provide an offensive springboard to release the strikers.

Nazon weighed in with a few valuable early season goals before departing. McNulty however, struggled to find the target despite being heralded by Robins as a 20 plus goals plus striker. Again, the City boss asked for patience and reiterated his belief in the marksman. On October 17th, City's ongoing flirtation with the elusive top six place received a blow when league new boys Forest Green Rovers won at the Ricoh. This eased pressure on the struggling newcomers and flashed a warning signal of a problem that threatened to derail our season.

City toiled desperately against teams near the bottom of the table, regularly scuppering the acca of many who like a bet and go on form. Paradoxically and in typical Cov fashion the higher placed and better an opponent looked, the more it seemed to suit the Sky Blues. Thus adding a new strain to the virus of inconsistency that had plagued us for decades.

A hammer blow occurred when Jones picked up a bad injury that ruled him out of the rest of the season. But McNulty began to find the target regularly and with it his confidence, revealing an astute first touch and ability to bring others into play. The two injuries ruling out key creative players opened the door for youngsters, Tom Bayliss and Jordan Shipley. Both grasped the opportunity with both hands, looking highly promising.

City went into new year still in a prominent position and pulled off an FA shock at the Ricoh by knocking out Premiership Stoke in the 3rd round. The result cost Potteries boss Mark Hughes his job. Millions of viewers who watched the highlights on Match of the Day were impressed by City and Jack Grimmer's brilliant winner. It took a trip to another Premiership team, Brighton, to end Sky Blue interest in the competition.

Slowly my medication was having positive effect, although I didn't feel strong enough to attend a game until we played Accrington at home. Every week I watched the results come in with with my Dad who was deteriorating ever more. He had now completely lost his ability to speak. If we were watching a football scores programme and I was on my iPad doing my writing, he'd clap his hands if a City goal update flashed up to draw my attention to the screen. Really heartbreaking. As we looked at the league table, I longed for City to end the no top six finish curse in what I knew would be his last season after over seventy years of following the club.

A fine CCFC community day offer of a fiver adult admission and free for kids brought over 22,000 in the Ricoh on a foul day to watch us play Stanley. I have long maintained football is too overpriced and unaffordable for some people. Such initiatives are therefore commendable and help those who have been priced out of attending matches. Sadly for City, a useful Accrington side who would ultimately finish champions, won 2-0 putting a dampener on what was already an exceedingly damp day weather wise.

This result together with a few other recent blips saw City slide out of the playoff places towards mid-table. It seemed the second half of the season misery jinx would again rear its ugly head. But Robins men were made of sterner stuff. After another reverse at Colchester they put an eight game unbeaten run together. McNulty now on fire, netted a hat trick in the crushing of Grimsby at home. City were now right back in contention though things were almost unbearably tight in the playoff race.

Easter is always a telling time in football and on Good Friday, the Sky Blues drew at Newport. This set them up nicely for the Easter Monday encounter with lowly Yeovil. The foundation of the season had been centred around a tough to breach rearguard that threatened to set a new club record for fewest goals conceded. So City were like a highly fancied boxer walking into a series of sucker punches as Yeovil went 3-0 up in fifteen minutes.

It finished 6-2 to the visitors. It's like City excel at finding new ways of messing with their fans heads with this extraordinary scoreline being right up there. Another blow came with defeat at playoff rivals Notts Country before highly rated young striker, Jordan Ponticelli came off the bench at Crawley to score twice as City bounced back with a 2-1 win. This made the home game with Stevenage the following Friday night at the Ricoh one of paramount importance.

Sadly, the day before that crucial encounter my father passed away. He was as hurt as anybody by the slide down the leagues his beloved Sky Blues had endured. I wanted City to go up more than ever now for him. God bless my Dad and McNulty then, as the ace goalscorer nicknamed Sparky scored twice in the first six minutes. City ran out comfortable 3-1 victors.

I put out an emotional tweet stating what had happened ending with, "That one's for you Dad." The response completely overwhelmed me. There were hundreds of replies stating condolences and support. Many from supporters of other clubs. Social media can be much maligned but I was so grateful for football Twitter showing kind hearts extend from people you've never met. A connection football makes like no other.

Fellow top six contenders Lincoln City came to the Ricoh the following Tuesday night for a fixture originally postponed thanks to the Midlands plunging into an artic weekend. It was like City froze again as the sudden outbreak of defensive frailties surfaced again in a 4-2 defeat. We still had a good chance but the penultimate hurdle, aptly at Cheltenham, was of paramount importance.

After twenty minutes the Sky Blues were three up. McNulty scored twice and went on to bag his second hat trick of the season. Youngsters Shipley and Bayliss both joined in the fun. Max Biamou also netted, just reward for a player who had become a fans favourite. He wasn't a regular scorer but proved a perfect foil for McNulty and when Biamou did find the net it was often in spectacular fashion.

The 6-1 demolition of Cheltenham meant just a single point was needed to make the playoffs in the final fixture. In a twist, opponents, Morecambe would arrive at the Ricoh needing only a draw to stay up and consign Barnet to non league football. Given that, only one result looked likely.

And so it proved. You could imagine Sunderland fans exploding with anger, screaming, "They're at it again!" With too much to lose, neither side committed greatly to attack and the sides played out a tame goalless draw. Job done for both sides but hard on Barnet. Their manager, Martin Allen had the end of his season ruined once before by City, 1987 if I remember correctly.

One of the most unwanted blights in club football had come to an end. After 48 seasons, Coventry had finished in the top six of a division again. Their first team to do so since 1969-70 when Noel Cantwell led the club into Europe. There were three points to spare in the end. At last, football result presenters would have to find another fascinating fact when showing a league table with City in the top six.

The two legged playoff semi final would be against Notts County with the first meeting at the Ricoh. This took place on a Saturday night due to Sky scheduling. The weather dealt a blow in the lead up to the game when there was a downpour of biblical proportions, soaking the playing surface. This would make City's preferred slick crisp passing game difficult and suit the more direct play of County.

A bright start by the home side gave way to a tight first half. This was followed by Kevin Nolan's men taking a second half lead. City were tottering but clung on. With three minutes remaining, Bayliss went on another driving run down the channel into the box where he went over from a challenge as the ball went out of play. The referee pointed to the spot, as Nolan and his players went ballistic.

McNulty who hit a post in the first half, cooly stroked home the spot kick. I didn't think it was a foul at first look and less so when I saw the replays. But you need a bit of luck. It reaffirms belief you're destined to succeed. Also, the defender didn't have to commit to the tackle. Bayliss was running up a cul de sac. If a defender goes to ground in the box he gives the officials a decision to make and sometimes they get it wrong.

The fiery Nolan didn't see it that way in an emotional after match rant come interview. He also complained about a stray elbow on an Country forward in the first half from excellent City defender, Tom Davis. The cameras bore him out on that one and Davis got a retrospective two match suspension ruling him out of the second encounter and final should we get there.

The following Friday night saw the Sky Blue army travel to Meadow Lane in full force and voice. For the first 45 minutes, City played some of their best football in years leaving the commentators drooling about how far we looked above our status. Several opportunities went begging but fine strikes from Biamou and McNulty, his 28th of the season, put City in command. But then just before the break, some slack defensive concentration led to Country pulling one back.

This made the second half a totally different proposition. County were back in it and fired up. City keeper Lee Bruge made one superb save to keep us in front. Then Nolan's head was cooking on gas mark six as County's Forte had a goal disallowed for offside when he was level. Good fortune helped fire up the Sky Blues determination. Biamou and

McNulty teamed up for the former to score his second and then Bayliss put the gloss on the scoreline.

City were going to Wembley again. Nolan bitterly berated the officials but for most of the 180 minute tie, City were by far the best side. I know I'm biased but for years we were plagued by bad luck at vital times. It had turned round. Even the best sides need the rub of the green and there was little doubt all the best football in that semi final had been played by the Sky Blues. Now we would meet Exeter, who had finished fourth.

"Just one game stands between Coventry's first promotion since 1967."

That was the next nauseous statistic trotted out on the sports news programmes. A bit misleading because we were in the old First Division for 34 consecutive years and obviously couldn't go any higher. Still, these things strengthen your resolve and I have to say I've never felt such positively buzzing off City fans as in the wait for the playoff final.

Due to the illness I've developed, I struggle stamina wise with long days out but there was no way I was going to miss out on this. So on Bank Holiday Monday 28th May, I boarded the National Express coach for Wembley with my mate's, Dave Whiting and Steve Slater. A chap and his young son, say around seven years old, sat in front of me on the coach. You could sense the excitement in the lad embarking out on a big adventure.

A sense of confident calm prevailed. The most concern I heard from fans was if they were going to get to The Green Man pub before it became a struggle to get served. This heightened when the driver missed the turnoff to Wembley stadium having to backtrack on himself. Thus committing one of the biggest sins you can bestow on football fans, forcing them to miss out on valuable drinking time.

I'd never been to the new Wembley before. The surrounds are a mix of impressive complexes and still in construction sites giving it a strange feel. I'd arranged to meet Dave Lanchbury in The Green Man which now took on mythical status as we tried in vain to find the place. Then like something out of a film, a little old lady appeared out of nowhere and told us the way. By the time, we got there the pub was full and they wouldn't let us in. An hour's worth of boozing wasted.

We eventually found an hotel bar before going for a stroll. By the fan park I bumped into my friend Andy Scobbie who also is a Parkinson's disease sufferer. I've been with him to a good few games over the years. A good loyal City supporter who like most, had become disillusioned with all the nonsense but put that behind him for what was shaping up to be a cracking day, result permitting.

My thoughts turned to another friend of mine and Andy's, John Scallan. John passed away a couple of years ago and would have loved Wembley that day. A ex Highfield Road steward he lived and breathed City. It's those sort of folk that football is about and that's sometimes forgotten amid the greed and mind numbing politics that blights the modern game.

City took 38,000 down to Wembley which I suspect is a record for a League Two playoff final. A hot day meant shirts only and the different replica tops on display was like a history of the club as retro mixed with new. Our desperation to find a bar without a queue led us to the Hilton Hotel and a few pints at £6.50 a throw.

"We've got Micheal Doyle with Kelly in the middle." Rang out time and time again in homage to the engine room of City's revival. The organisation and security in and around Wembley I found first class. With seats up in the Gods, we embarked on the several escalators long journey to the top tier. After sampling more beer in the stadium bars for research purposes of course, we made our way to our seats.

Exeter were outnumbered by around 3 to 1 and the support from the City fans was fantastic. For big games I always get that nervous butterflies in your stomach feeling. A drab goalless first half didn't help. We went back to the bar but gave up still waiting to get served as the second half started. The decision to return our seats without another pint paid instant dividends. From 25 yards out, the magnificent first touch of defender Jordan Willis was bettered by his second as he curled a long range stunner into the net. Cue limbs everywhere, stranger hugging stranger, like it says in that advert, priceless.

Just five minutes later, our other Jordan, young Shipley, made it two with a deflected effort. City were now playing some irresistible stuff, they'd peaked at exactly the right time. I thought of my Dad of how he'd have loved this and welled up a bit. Then I pulled myself together. This day was one of celebration. Confirmed in the 68th minute when an exquisite set up by McNulty led to another spectacular curler from outside the box courtesy of Jack Grimmer.

For once you could relax and enjoyed the feeling. Exeter got a late consolation but this day belonged to the people of Coventry. After so many dark days the sun shone brightly in aptly a sky of pure blue as City went up to collect the trophy. The scoreboard using Sky footage flashed up the image of the ecstatic John Sillett, drawing one of the biggest cheers of the day. In contrast to the next face on screen, that of Fisher met by boos.

Later, watching the highlights on telly, I saw the lesser spotted Joy Seppala also in the directors box bizarrely sitting next to a vicar. Even God it seemed was rooting for us that day. Another City anthem Twist and Shout burst out everywhere as we made our way down what must be hundreds of steps. Truly a stairway to a heavenly afternoon complete with the clergy.

Of course nothing goes entirely smoothly in the world of the Sky Blues. Sure enough, our coach broke down on way home. We all got off because it was hot and stuffy inside. So we stood on the hard shoulder waiting for the replacement to arrive. Thankfully we were only about twenty miles from Cov when the engine packed up. Numerous vehicles drove past, honking their horns, waving City scarves at us.

Two days later, thousands more fans lined the streets and gathered in the City Centre for the victory parade. The huge turnout illustrated how success starved the club had been but again, also the vast potential. You never know quite what something means to you until you come close to losing it. The years of decline may have been heartbreaking but in another way it had reminded City fans the club held a unique place in those hearts.

I have come to the conclusion that everything about a football club is temporary and replaceable apart from its soul which is permanent. Owners are just leasing custodians, some more responsible than others. The players, paid representatives. Fans who give a lifetime's allegiance to their team leave their legacy to future generations, like with my Dad and the young awestruck kid on the bus. We trust them to guard this inheritance well as we did.

Supporting your local club is a truly wonderful thing. It often brings far more pain than joy. But those little nuggets of gold you occasionally find on the footballing sands, make it all worthwhile. Bringing a sense of community and belonging that the causal glory-hunter could never begin to comprehend. The real believers are everywhere. From those who voluntarily give up time to help their club to the diehard addicts who even question their own sanity at their commitment to their team's cause.

Coventry City have been to the brink of oblivion. But the very symbol of the City itself is the Phoenix rising. Just as it did through the collapse of key industries, readjusting and reinventing to survive. Just as it did through the horrors of the Coventry Blitz, rebuilding and finding reconciliation in the wake of unthinkable devastation. A City with a cathedral to spare and one hell of a story to tell.

In many ways that tale is told in part at least, like many cities and towns through its football club. A story of changing times, challenged loyalties, questioned faith. Times when evolution feels more like backward revolution. But football matters, is cherished and loved because at its best, at its core, it has feel of family, the camaraderie of good friends, the tingling of a unique time spent with a loved one.

The game has changed. At times we question its integrity. But people remain it's identity. Jimmy Hill once said, "You can beat a team, but you can't beat a team and a City." Those last few days in May 2018 proved his words right. As I've found, as Coventry fans have found, cherish what you have, you never know when you might lose it. As local band The Enemy sang, we'll live and die in these towns. It's what we do in between that counts.

And while you could argue for forty eight years of hurt in league football the Sky Blues achieved nothing, they still provided a lot of memories. Days on which lifelong friendships were formed, parental legacies handed down, all kinds of emotions good and bad to learn from. Because these are the unheralded trophies in football, the feelings that make it all worthwhile.

Football is about the next game, more than the last one. Another chance for renewal, eternal optimism when you really should know better. I suppose in a way that's the game's main appeal, you can retain that innocence, there's always hope tomorrow will be a better day. At last Coventry fans have a taste of what that feels like. When you can finally picture a brighter horizon. Like looking at the world through Sky Blue eyes.

Printed in Great Britain
by Amazon

42417989R00090